Practice like you play.

Play like you practice.

Copyright © 2019 by 3 Wise Teachers, LLC

All rights reserved. No part of this publication may be reproduced, distributed, or transmitted in any form or by any means, including photocopying, recording, or other electronic or mechanical methods, without the prior written permission of the publisher, except in the case of brief quotations embodied in critical reviews and certain other noncommercial uses permitted by copyright law. For permission requests, write to the publisher, addressed "Attention: Permissions Coordinator," at the address below.

3 Wise Teachers, LLC
202 Crawford Road
Hillsborough, NC 27278
www.3WiseTeachers.com

Ordering Information:
Quantity sales. Special discounts are available on quantity purchases by corporations, associations, and others. For details, contact the publisher at the address above.

Printed in the United States of America

**Free Math Exam
25 Questions
Visit www.LearnTestPass.com**

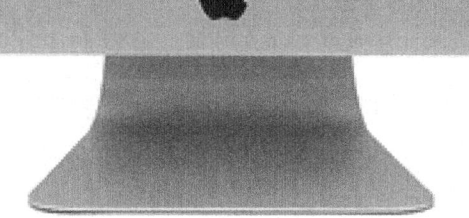

3 Wise Teachers

North Carolina—State Only Exam Review (new edition coming soon)

North Carolina—Comprehensive Exam Review (new book to be released soon)

Do you have a license in another state? We are looking to expand our offerings. Give us a call at 919-391-8180.

We have partnered with Learn Test Pass to offer a free 25 question math exam online. Make sure to check out the details at the end of the book.

Easy to Follow Problems

This workbook is designed to give you examples of how to work actual real estate mathematics problems, that you would encounter as a real estate broker. Problems are stated, and then solved so that you can follow the steps involved.

BACK TO BASICS

Real Estate Math involves mostly being able to add, subtract, multiply and divide. Some problems will require you to change a percent to a decimal. Others will ask for the area of shapes (lots). Read the question carefully and multiple times.

These are primarily word problems, because they are written in a narrative form. And as such, require you to read the problem carefully. Determine what is being asked and what is just filler or unnecessary. Always, always try and draw a diagram or picture of the problem, make a column, a list. Re-write the problem in an outline form that will help you understand the problem. Draw a diagram or make columns that separate information into a format you can understand. There will be problems for you to solve. Always read the question carefully.

Ok, here we go….

TABLE of CONTENTS

Topic	Page
Formulas / Measurements / The Basic	1
Property Taxation & Assessment	4
Area Calculation - Lots	7
Rectangular Survey Method	11
Square Yards	12
Excise Tax	15
Agency Commission	16
Sales Price Need for Seller to Net	20
Living Area – Square Footage	22
Mortgage Math – Points, Fees, LTV, Factors	25
Simple Interest – Over Life of Loan / Loan Comparison	29
Amortization & Debt Service (Mortgage)	31
Mortgage Qualification	34
Prorations – Interim Int, Accrued, Property Tax, Rent & HOA	38
Mini-Closing Problems	50
Valuation – Sales Comparison Approach	55
Valuation – Cost Approach	61
Valuation – Income Approach – Income Capitalization	63
Valuation – Income Approach – Gross Rent (Income) Multiplier	66
Federal Taxation (no calculations)	69
Gain on Sale – Total or Percentage	70
Gain on Equity – Total or Percentage	71
Property Management – Fee Calculation	72
Percentage Lease (Retail)	75
Solutions	77
Practice Exam 1 / Solution	106 / 115
Practice Exam 2 / Solution	123 / 132

FORMULAS & MEASUREMENTS:

1 Square Foot = 12" x 12" (or 144 Square Inches)

    1 Cubic Foot = 12" x 12" x 12" (or 1,728 cubic inches or 1 cubic foot)

    1 Yard = 3 feet (36 inches)

    1 Square Yard = 9 Square Feet (3' x 3')

    1 Cubic Yard = 27 Cubic Feet (3' x 3' x 3')

1 Acre = 43,560 square feet (you must remember this)

    There are 36 square miles in a Township

1 Square Mile = 640 Acres (Government Survey Method) (each section)

    Each section can be divided. 640 ÷ denominator(s)

    Area of a Square or Rectangle = width x depth

    Area of a Triangle = ½ base x height

Property Tax NC = Assessed Value ÷ 100 x Tax Rate
Property Tax National = Assessed Value ÷ 1000 x Mills Rate
Excise Tax = Sold Price ÷ 500 rounded to the next whole dollar

Commission = Sold Price x % Commission

Capitalization Rate of Return

    Cap Rate = NOI ÷ Value

    Value = NOI ÷ Cap Rate

    NOI = Value x Cap Rate

Depreciation of Building
    Straight Line Per Year = New Value ÷ Useful Life

    Accumulated Depreciation = SL Depreciation x Effective Age

Introduction to Real Estate Math

To be successful in the math portion of the real estate prelicensing course exam and the State & National Licensing exams, you will need to be familiar with the many types of math problems that you will be introduced to in this course. This workbook is to be used in conjunction with the course syllabus, to help you focus on the type of math that is covered on the exam at that time.

Keep in mind that math is between 15 to 20% of the exam. You will be allowed to use a simple non-programmable, battery operated hand held calculator.

When testing, it is very important that you read the entire problem carefully and determine what you are solving the problem for. Be careful to pay attention to instructions at the end of problems, such as rounding to nearest $100, or if the answer is a %.

For exam purposes, and for the problems in this workbook, you will use the Statutory or Banker's Year (360 day year / 30 day months), unless otherwise stated.

Introduction to the Triangle Method

The Triangle Method is a helpful visual tool to use to solve math problems by dividing them into 3 components: 1 – Part, 2 – Whole, 3 – Rate. The Part can be a number that is larger or smaller than the whole, depending on the rate. The Whole is the number that is the original cost/price/size in the problem. The rate is related to profit or loss as compared to the whole (1). If there is a profit, the rate will be 1 + % profit. (ie: 30% profit, rate = 1 + 0.30 = 1.3). If there is a loss, the rate will be 1 - % loss. (ie: 20% loss, rate = 1-0.20 = 0.8). The part will reflect that profit or loss in comparison to the whole.

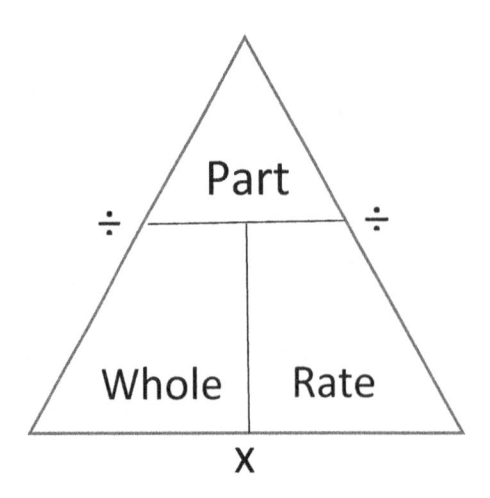

To use this method, you have to have 2 variables and you solve for the 3rd one. If you are given a Part and a Whole, you will divide the Part by the Whole to get the Rate. If you are given Part and Rate, you also divide the Part by the Rate to get the Whole. If you are given Whole and Rate, you will multiply these two to get the Part.

Example 1. Jane sold her house for $120,000. She originally purchased the home for $100,000. What is her percentage of profit?

Part = 20,000. Whole = 100,000. Part/Whole = 0.2 or 20% profit.

Example 2. Cathy paid $150,000 for her home, then later sold it for $130,000. What was Cathy's percentage of loss?

Part = -20,000. Whole = 150,000. Part/Whole = 0.1333 or 13.3% loss.

Example 3. Bob sold his home for $225,000, which netted him a profit of 30%. What was his original purchase price?

Part – 225,000. Rate = 1 + 0.30 = 1.3. Part/Rate = $173,076.92

Example 4. Jamen bought 5 acres of land for $17,000 per acre. If he subdivides the land into 15 lots and sells them for $7,500 each, what will be his percent of profit?

Old = 5 X $17,000 = $85,000. New = 15 X $7,500 = $112,500.
Gain = $112,500 - $85,000 = $27,500

Part/Whole: $27,500 / $85,000 = .3235 or 32.35% profit.

Example 5. A seller asks her broker to list her house for 20% more than what she originally paid for it. The house was listed and sold for 7% less than the asking price. If the seller sold her house for $195,000, how much did she originally pay?

The sales price represents 93% of the list price (100% - 7%). A percentage can be expressed as a decimal – so 93% = .93.

The list price represents a 20% increase from the purchase price (100% + 20%). A percentage can be expressed as a decimal – so 120% = 1.2.

Part = $195,000. Rate = .93. Part ÷ Rate = $209,677 Listed Price
Part = $209,667. Rate = 1.20. Part ÷ Rate = $174,731

PROPERTY TAXATION AND ASSESSMENT

Tax Rate and Calculations:

North Carolina uses the formula of a tax rate per $100 of assessed valuation.

National uses a tax formula based on "mils" which is $1000 of assessed valuation.

Example: Use an Assessed Value of $185,500.

- North Carolina, use a tax rate of $1.50.

   $185,500 ÷ 100 = 1,855

   1,855 x 1.50 = $2,782.50 = Tax Bill

- National Uses the "Mils" method, use 15 mils

   $185,500 ÷ 1000 = 185.5

   185.5 x 15 = $2,782.50 = Tax Bill

North Carolina = A problem will give the tax rate as $X.XX per $100 of assessed valuation - Divide the assessed value by 100 and multiply by the tax rate
National = A problem will give the tax rate as XX.X Mills per $1,000 of assessed value – Divide assessed value by 1,000 and multiply by the mills rate.

A property located in the city will pay both city and county taxes.
A property located in the county will pay only county taxes.

Example 1. What is the assessed value of a tract of land located outside of city limits if the current tax bill is $2,775? The county tax rate is $0.65 and the city tax rate is $0.92.

Assessed Value ÷ 100 X Tax Rate = Taxes for Year
So… Taxes YR ÷ Tax Rate = Assessed Value … Then multiply by $100
$2,775 ÷ $0.65 = $4,269.2308 X $100 = $426,923.08

Example 2. Sarah's house is located in the city, where the assessed value has been set at 75% of the market value. What is her monthly tax bill if the city tax rate is $1.34 and the county rate is $0.95 and the house has a fair market value of $229,000?

Assessed Value ÷ 100 X Tax Rate = Taxes for Year
Assessed Value: $229,000 X 75% = $171,750
Tax YR: $171,750 ÷ 100 X $2.29 = $3,933.08
Tax per Month: $3,933.08 ÷ 12 = $327.76

Example 3. What is the annual tax of a property if the assessed value is $165,000 and the tax rate is 25 mills?

Assessed Value ÷ 1,000 X Mills Rate = Taxes for Year
$165,000 ÷ 1,000 X 25 = $4,125

Example 4. Shirley's house is located in a city with a mill rate of 33. If assessed value is 85% of the market value and the tax bill for the year is $3,100, what is the market value?

Assessed Value ÷ 1,000 X Mills Rate = Taxes for Year

To calculate Market Value: Tax for Year AV ÷ Mills Rate X 1,000 ÷ 85%
$3,100 ÷ 33 = $93.9393 X $1,000 = $93,939.39 ÷ 85% = $110,516.93

Problems for you to Solve (solutions page 77):

1. A owner's assessed tax value is $185,800 and the property tax rate is $1.50 for a property located in North Carolina. What are the annual taxes on the property?

    a. $2,780.50
    b. $2,787.00
    c. $2,790.00
    d. $2,800.00

2. A property owner sold his waterfront house/lot for $245,000. The County assessed the property at $235,500. The property is located in the city limits. County tax rate is $1.35 and City tax rate is $.62. What are the annual taxes?

    a. $1,460.10
    b. $3,179.25
    c. $4,639.35
    d. $4,826.50

3. The Jones home has an assessed value of $100,000 in a locality where the tax rate is $1.45 per $100. What is their monthly payment for taxes, rounded to nearest dollar?

    a. $ 83.00
    b. $ 100.00
    c. $ 121.00
    d. $1,450.00

4. Jim's home, located in the city of Raleigh, NC received an assessed value of $155,000 and the land an assessed value of $30,000. If county taxes are $0.85 and city taxes are $1.02, what would Jim's tax bill be rounded to the nearest dollar?

    a. $1,573.00
    b. $1,887.00
    c. $2,899.00
    d. $3,460.00

5. Kim's house is located within the city limits and has a market value of $240,000. The local tax office assessed her property at 75% and the tax rate per $100 of $0.95 for the City and $0.35 for the County. What are her annual taxes for this property?

    a. $1,710
    b. $2,280
    c. $2,340
    d. $3,120

6. A parcel of land is being taxed at a rate of 25 mils. Assuming that it has a market value of $175,000 and is being assessed at 70%. What would the annual tax bill be rounded to the nearest dollar?

   a. $1,225
   b. $3,063
   c. $4,375
   d. $4,900

AREA PROBLEMS – Lots and Cost

Important Dimensions:

Square Feet in an Acre = 43,560
Linear Feet in a Mile = 5,280
Acreage in a Section = 640

Area problems may require you to work with the square footage of a lot, acreage or front footage. It is important to read the question carefully to determine the unit of measurement.

Square footage is determined by taking the length X width. For example a lot measures 150' X 250'. What is the square footage of the lot?

   150 x 250 = 37,500

A question may ask about the acreage of a lot. It is vital that you recall an acre has 43,560 square feet (4 blue hair ladies driving 35 in a 60). What is the acreage of the above lot?

   37,500 ÷ 43,560 = 0.86

A question may require you to determine the list price or sales price of a lot based upon square footage or acreage. Based on the above lot, if similar property has sold for $35,000 what is the probable sales price of the lot?

   0.86 x $35,000 = $30,130.85

You may also be asked to calculate the cost per front foot. The first call number given for lot dimensions is known as the front footage. What is the cost per front foot for this lot?

$30,130.85 ÷ 150 = $200.87 per front foot.

In rare circumstances you may be asked to calculate the perimeter of a lot. Perimeter is the length or distance around an object, not the square footage inside the lot. If we need to find the amount of fencing needed for this property, we add the lengths of each side. The perimeter is determined by adding the linear feet.

Example 1. Paul owns a lot with 12.5 acres. He plans to subdivide the land into quarter acre lots. 25% of the property will be used for roads, parks and green space. How many buildable lots will Paul be able to sell?

Square footage of undivided lot: 12.5 acres X 43,560 = 544,500 sqft.
Usable Land: 100% - 25% = 75%
Subdividable Land: 544,500 X 75% = 408,375
Lot Square Footage: 43,560 ÷ 4 = 10,890 square feet
Number of Lots: 408,375 ÷ 10,890 = 37.5 or 37 lots

Example 2. Shawn owns a property that is 2 miles X 350'. How many acres does Shawn own?

One mile = 5,280 feet so 2 miles = 10,560 feet
Square Footage of Lot: 10,560' X 350' = 3,696,000
Acres: 3,696,000 ÷ 43,560 = 84.84 acres (don't round up acreage)

Example 3. A lot measures 300' X 1500'. Similar lots have sold for $65,000 per acre. What is the value of the lot rounded to the nearest dollar?

Lot Square Footage: 300' X 1,500' = 450,000 sqft.
Acres: 450,000 ÷ 43,560 = 10.3305 acres
Value: 10.3305 X $65,000 = $671,487.60 or $671,488

Problems for you to Solve (solutions page 78):

1. A lot measures 150 feet X 250 feet. How many acres does this lot have?

    a. 0.86 acres
    b. 0.90 acres
    c. 1.74 acres
    d. 2.00 acres

2. A rectangular lot measures 250' X 750'. The buyer paid $195 per front foot. How much did the property sell for?

    a. $187,500
    b. $146,250
    c. $ 83,500
    d. $ 48,750

3. A lot contains 0.9 acres. What is the depth of the lot if the front measures 150 feet?

    a. 216.36'
    b. 261.36'
    c. 322.67'
    d. 323.67'

4. A rectangular lot measures 200' x 300'. Property in the area is selling for $150,000 per acre. If the broker gets an 8% commission on the price of the property, how much will they make, rounded to the nearest dollar.

    a. $15,692
    b. $16,529
    c. $16,730
    d. $19,243

5. A buyer purchased a lot that is one-mile square and another that measures 511.23' x 511.23'. At a cost of $2,000 an acre, how much did she pay in total for both lots?

   a. $1,292,000
   b. $1,373,435
   c. $1,733,435
   d. $1,922,000

6. Two adjoining lots contain the same front footage. Lot A is 900 feet deep and Lot B is 780 feet deep. If Lot A contains 3.45 acres, how many acres are in Lot B? (round to the nearest whole number).

   a. 2.99 acres
   b. 3.98 acres
   c. 5.56 acres
   d. 16.11 acres

7. A tract of land measuring 165' x 350' deep recently sold for $138,600. What is the price per front foot (round to the nearest whole dollar)?

   a. $141
   b. $269
   c. $396
   d. $840

8. A tract of land measuring 750' x 825' is divided into two equal tracts by a stream that runs diagonally through the property. How many acres are in each portion of the property?

   a. 14.10 acres
   b. 10.65 acres
   c. 7.10 acres
   d. 3.55 acres

9. A buyer recently purchased a lot containing 0.3817 acres. How many square feet does this lot contain?

   a. 24,275
   b. 21,875
   c. 17,825
   d. 16,627

AREA PROBLEMS - RECTANGULAR SURVEY METHOD
(Not Used in North Carolina)

Townships are laid out in 6 x 6 grid that total 36 sections. They are numbered starting at the top right with #1 and the top left box is #6, second row down on the left is #7 and second row down on the right is #12, next row down on the right is #13, and so on.

Each section is 640 acres or one square mile. The township has 36 square miles.

You always calculate by taking the denominator of the fraction given and divide into 640. This is because you are further dividing a section into quarters or halves to identify a parcel of land.

Example 1. How many acres are in the NE1/4 of the SW1/4 of the NW1/4 of a given section?

Acreage: 640 ÷ 4 ÷ 4 ÷ 4 = 10 acres.

Example 2. Taylor sold the SE1/4 of the NW 1/4 of Section 6 and the N 1/2 of Section 5 for $3,000 an acre. How much did Taylor receive for the land?

Section 6 acreage = 640 ÷ 4 ÷ 4 = 40 acres
Section 5 acreage = 640 ÷ 2 = 320
Total Acreage: 40 + 320 = 360
Sales Price: 360 X $3,000 = $1,080,000

Example 3. How many acres are in the NE1/4 of the SW1/4 of the N1/2 of a given section?

Acreage: 640 ÷ 4 ÷ 4 ÷ 2 = 20 acres

Problems for you to Solve (solutions page 80):

1. John purchases the SW1/4 of the SW1/4 of the NW1/4 of section 14 and the NE1/4 of the SE1/4 of the SE1/4 of section 15. How many acres does John Own?

    a. 10 acres
    b. 20 acres
    c. 40 acres
    d. 320 acres

2. Kelly purchased the S1/2 of the SW1/4 of the NE1/4 of section 17 and 10 acres. She paid $35,000 per acre. What was the purchase price of the property?

    a. $ 350,000
    b. $ 700,000
    c. $1,050,000
    d. $1,750,000

3. How many acres does the N1/2 of the N1/2 of the SW1/4 of section 21 contain?

    a. 10 acres
    b. 20 acres
    c. 40 acres
    d. 80 acres

SQUARE YARDS DISCUSSION AND PROBLEMS

Typically, we use calculations of square yards for estimating the cost of carpet, concrete, topsoil, and some types of flooring. It is more common to associate calculating square yards when measuring a room for new carpet, because carpet is sold by the square yard, and not square feet.

Same calculations could be performed to calculate the cost of a concrete patio where the question may relate to the cost per square yard cubic yard. It is important to make sure that the numbers you are multiplying are the same unit of measurement (inches, feet, yards, etc.).

How do we calculate square yards?

There are 3 feet in a yard. A square yard measures 3' X 3'. There are 9 square feet in a square yard, 3' X 3' = 9 square feet.

Example 1. A large master bedroom measures 16 feet long by 12 feet wide. How many square yards of carpet would need to be purchased?

Square feet: 16' x 12' = 192 Square Feet (sf)
Square yard: 192 / 9 = 21.33 square yards

Example 2. Mary is going to replace the carpet in the house she and her husband are planning to put on the market. The carpet costs $16.11/sy from Home Depot. There is also an installation charge of $45/hour labor. How much will the carpet cost if the room is 478 square feet and it takes 1 labor hour per 15 square yards of carpet?

Square Feet to Square Yards: 478 sq.ft. / 9' = 53.11 square yards.
Carpet Cost: 53.11 square yards x $16.11/sy = $855.62
Labor Hours: 53.11 / 15 = 3.54 hours.
Labor Cost: 3.54 X $45/hr = $159.33.
Total Job Cost: $855.62 + $159.33 = $1,014.95.

Problems for you to Solve (solutions page 80):

1. Joy is purchasing a house and plans to replace the carpet in the living and family rooms. The living room measures 22' x 17' and the family room is 16' x14'. How many square yards of carpet will she need?

    a. 598.00
    b. 224.00
    c. 66.44
    d. 22.15

2. Ed and Mary are preparing their house for resale and are considering replacing carpet in the family room and den. The family room carpet will have a lot of traffic on it and they are looking for carpet that is durable. The cost of this type of carpet runs $18 per square yard installed. The den is a cozy room and they want a shag rug that costs $25 per square yard installed. What is the cost to install the carpet when the family room is 22' x 15' and the den is 15' x 13', rounded to the nearest dollar?

   a. $ 542
   b. $ 660
   c. $1,062
   d. $1,202

3. Tom and Sandy will be adding a concrete patio with special flashing to make it look like stone. The concrete costs $45 per square yard and the flashing is $25 per square foot. How much will the project cost if the patio is 25' x 15' and Labor is $935?

   a. $12,185
   b. $11,250
   c. $10,310
   d. $ 9,375

4. Joan is having linoleum installed in her new kitchen because it is hypo-allergenic. She is purchasing this product from Lowes at a cost of $47.35/sy installed. The kitchen has a total of 259 square feet. How much will the project cost, rounded to the nearest dollar?

   a. $1,126
   b. $1,363
   c. $1,637
   d. $2,877

EXCISE TAX

Excise taxes are typically paid by the Seller at Closing. In North Carolina they are charged as $1 per $500 of sales price. For testing purposes you may be asked the steps take to calculate, without an actual math problem – round up sales price to the nearest $500 or $1,000 and then divide by $500. Otherwise when performing a math calculation take the sale price of the property, divide by 500 and then rounded to the next whole dollar (ex: $140.01 = $141).

Example 1. $74,000 cash sale

74,000 ÷ 500 = $148

Example 2. $274,100 FHA sale

274,100 ÷ 500 = $548.20, rounded up to $549

Example 3. $474,700 loan assumption sale

474,700 ÷ 500 = $949.40 round up to $950

Problems for you to Solve (solutions page 81):

1. A home sold for $103,250. What is the amount of excise tax to be paid by the seller?

    a. $206
    b. $207
    c. $103
    d. $104

2. A home was listed for $377,500 and ultimately closed for $365,000. What is the amount of excise tax to be paid by the seller?

    a. $365
    b. $378
    c. $730
    d. $755

3. A home is listed for $295,000 and sells for 6% less than the asking price. What is the amount of excise tax to be paid by the seller?

    a. $590
    b. $555
    c. $295
    d. $278

AGENCY COMMISSION

How to calculate commission and splits between brokers and firms.

Sales price X commission rate = Commission

When using the T-Bar: (Sales Price – Whole, Commission – Part, Com. Rate – Rate)

Be careful with seller's agent vs selling agent. The **seller's agent** is the listing agent. The **selling agent** is the buyer's agent. Total compensation is paid to the listing firm and then split according to the listing contract with the cooperating real estate firm that wrote the offer.

Example 1. A seller agreed to a 6% commission on the sale of their house. If the house sold for $240,000, how much was the commission?

$240,000 x 0.06 (6% as a decimal) = $14,400 Gross Commission

Example 2. A property sold for $225,000 at a commission rate of 6%. The firm collects a 6% franchise fee from total commission and then pays the agent 55% of the remainder, how much did the agent make on the transaction?

$225,000 x .06 = $13,500 Gross Commission

$13,500 x .06 = $810 Franchise Fee

$13,500 - $810 = $12,690 Commission less Franchise Fee

$12,690 x .55 = $6,979.50 Agent Commission

Example 3. The listing agreement calls for a broker to make a 7% of the first $150,000 of sales price, 6% on the next $150,000 and 5% on the balance. What is the total commission if the house sells for $380,000?

Commission at 7% of $150,000 x .07 = $10,500

Commission at 6% of $150,000 x .06 = $ 9,000

380,000 – 300,000 = $80,000 x .05   = $ 4,000

Total Commission is $23,500

Example 4. Christy sold a property for a 5% commission rate with another firm, for $240,000. The listing firm agrees to a 50/50 split on commission. Christy's firm will charge a 5% franchise fee on all earned commissions and then pay her 65% on the balance. How much did Christy earn on this transaction?

$240,000 x .05   = $12,000 Gross Commission

$12,000 x .50   = $ 6,000 each firm's split

$ 6,000 x .95   = $ 5,700 commission after franchise fee

$ 5,700 x .65   = $ 3,705 Christy's share

Example 5. A property sold for $2.5 million with the seller agreeing to pay the listing agent 6% commission on the first million, 5% commission on the second million and 4% commission on the remainder. How much did the listing agent earn?

$1,000,000 X 6% = $60,000
$1,000,000 X 5% = $50,000
  $500,000 X 4% = $20,000

Total Commission: $60,000 + $50,000 + $20,000 = $130,000

Problems for you to Solve (solutions page 82):

1. A broker sold a house for $110,000 and acted as dual agent in the transaction. The commission was 6% and his listing firm charges a 6% franchise fee. The agent splits commission on a 70/30 basis. How much did the agent receive? (round up to the nearest whole dollar)

    a. $6,600
    b. $6,204
    c. $4,620
    d. $4,343

2. A home recently sold for $480,000. The listing firm said they would split the 7% commission with the buyer agents firm. The buyer's agent splits compensation on a 70/30 basis. In addition to commission the buyer's agent received a $1,000 bonus for being the procuring cause of the sale. The buyer's agent independent contract agreement does not require bonuses to be split with the brokerage. How much did the Buyer's agent make in the transaction?

    a. $10,500
    b. $11,760
    c. $12,760
    d. $16,800

3. A real estate broker listed a property for $95,000 and sold the property for $90,000. The seller paid 7% commission to her employing broker, with 60% paid to her by her brokerage. How much did the agent receive?

    a. $2,520
    b. $2,646
    c. $3,780
    d. $5,400

4. A house listed for $84,900. The seller received $71,424 after paying a broker commission of 7%. What was the selling price of the property?

   a. $76,424
   b. $76,800
   c. $78,957
   d. $91,290

5. John sold his house on November 12th for $365,000. He paid the listing firm a commission of 6.5% of the first $100,000; 5% of the second $100,000 and the remaining balance at 4.5%. The commission was equally split between the Listing and Selling firm. The buyer's agent will receive 70% of her side of the transaction. How much is the Buyer Agent's fee, rounded to the nearest dollar?

   a. $ 6,623
   b. $ 7,425
   c. $ 9,462
   d. $13,248

6. Tiffany, a licensed broker with Excel Realty sold a commercial property for $4.6 million. The seller agreed to pay 7% on the first million, 6% on the second million and 4% for the remain of the sales price. How much compensation did Excel Realty receive?

   a. $104,000
   b. $130,000
   c. $234,000
   d. $322,000

SALES PRICE NEEDED FOR SELLER TO NET $X

It is common that you will need to calculate the sales price that is needed for the seller to net a certain amount of money while paying off his/her loan and the related closing expenses. This can be accomplished in 3 steps.

Step 1: Add up seller know expenses. Note that the seller typically pays C,D&E – commission, deed preparation and excise tax. Commission remains the unknown amount – since it is based on the sales price, which is what we are trying to calculate.

Step 2: Calculate the percentage that the above number represents. The sales price = 100% of the figure we are trying to calculate. Subtract the amount of commission from 100% and this will give you the percentage that the number above represents. Example: Commission is 7%, then the sales price less commission represents 93% of the sales price.

Step 3: Take the seller known expenses and divide by the percentage calculated above.

Example 1. A seller wants to net $45,000 and has the following expenses:
- Closing Costs - $4,000
- Loan Payoff - $218,000
- Commission – 6%
- Deed Preparation - $150

What would the house need to sell for in order for the seller to reach his/her goal, rounded to the nearest hundred?

Step 1 - Seller Knowns: $45,000 + $4,000 + $218,000 + $150 = $267,150
Step 2 - % of SP: SP 100% - Commission 6% = 94%
Step 3 - Sales Price: $267,150 ÷ 94% = $284,202.12 or $284,200

When using the T-Bar or Triangle: All of Seller expenses = Part, 100% -commission rate = rate. Divide (Part/Rate) to get the whole or sales price needed.

Example 2. Angela wishes to net $25,000 from the sale of her house. She needs to pay off her loan of $121,900, miscellaneous costs of $3,500, and a commission of 6%. What should the selling price be on the property?

Step 1 - Seller Known Expenses: $25,000 + $121,900 + $3,500 = $150,500.
Step 2 - % of SP: SP 100% - 6% = 94% (Convert 94% to a decimal 0.94)
Step 3 - Sale Price: $150,500 ÷ 0.94 = $160,000

Problems for you to Solve (solutions page 83):

1. A seller wants to net $85,000 from the sale of her home. The closing costs are estimated to be $2,500 and the commission to be paid is 6 percent. There is an existing loan of $50,000 that must be paid off at closing. What must the house sell for if the seller is to receive her desired net, rounded to the nearest hundred?

    a. $129,700
    b. $145,800
    c. $146,300
    d. $147,500

2. A seller wants to net $45,000 from the sale of her home. The closing costs are estimated to be $3,000 and the commission to be paid is 7 percent. There is an existing loan of $250,000 that must be paid off at closing. What must the house sell for if the seller is to receive his desired net, rounded to the nearest hundred?

    a. $277,100
    b. $298,000
    c. $320,400
    d. $398,000

3. Bruce is interested in selling his home if he can net $75,000 from the sale. He has a mortgage balance of $223,500, seller closing costs of $5,000 and will pay 7% to the listing broker. Bruce has an assumable loan that will cost the buyer 1% of the loan balance as an assumption fee, which would be paid to the bank. What must the sales price for the house be for Bruce to net the desired amount, rounded to the nearest hundred?

    a. $245,700
    b. $286,300
    c. $321,700
    d. $326,300

4. Carla is interested in selling her home if she can net $45,000 from the sale. Her current mortgage balance is $175,900. The sale would have the following expenses, paid by the typical party:

   * Deed Preparation $150   * Mortgage Cancel. $50   * Loan Orig. $2,000
         * Commission 5%   * Other Seller Closing Costs $7,000

   What must the sales price for the house be for Carla to net the desired amount, rounded to the nearest hundred?

   a. $192,700
   b. $239,500
   c. $240,100
   d. $242,200

LIVING AREA – SQUARE FOOTAGE

Recall that living area must be heated, finished and directly accessible. A garage, carport, deck, stoop or unfinished storage would not be included in the living area.

A house has dimensions of 42' x 36'. Remember length times width = square feet. 42' x 36' = 1,512 sf. When you measure a house you are calculating the outside area to give you the heated square feet of the house. You have to deduct the square footage for a garage and/or porch, areas that are not heated.

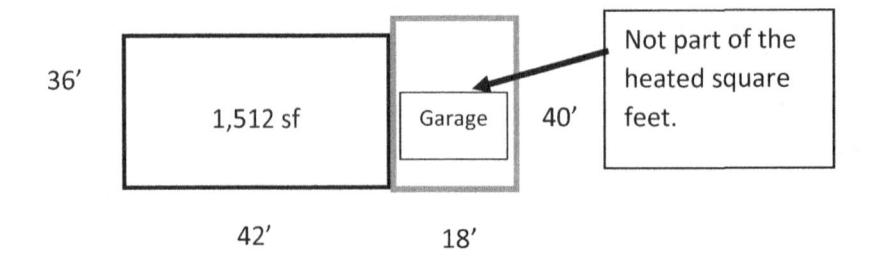

36' | 1,512 sf | Garage | 40' | Not part of the heated square feet.

42'   18'

In addition to rectangular homes, you may need to calculate the area of a triangle. When calculating the area of a triangle, we take the Base times the Height divided by 2.
42' x 36' ÷ 2 = 756 sf.

36'

756 sf

42'

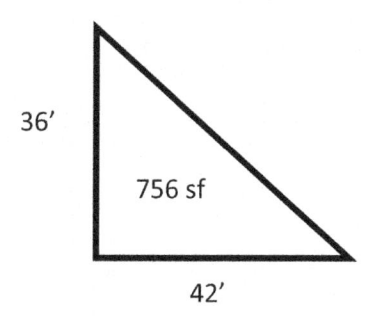

Area problems may require you to calculate the cost of a home or what the cost per square foot of a home is based upon the purchase price. To determine the cost per square foot – take the purchase price and divide by square footage.

In rare circumstance you may need to calculate the area of a trapezoid. The formula to calculate the area of a trapezoid is Area = ½ (base1 +base2) X height.

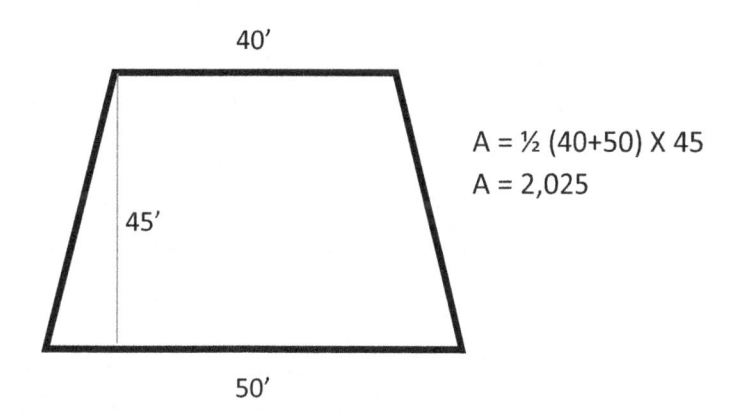

40'

45'

50'

A = ½ (40+50) X 45
A = 2,025

Problems for you to Solve (solutions page 84):

1. A husband and wife purchased a house that cost $325,000 by obtaining a $287,500 mortgage. The home has 2,300 square feet of heated living space. What is the cost per square foot?

    a. $125.00 / sf
    b. $141.30 / sf
    c. $175.62 / sf
    d. $707.69 / sf

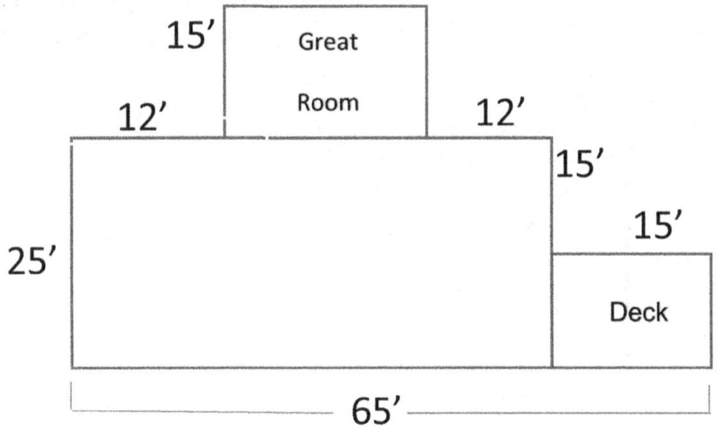

2. Using the diagram above, what is the living area square footage of the home?

   a. 1,640
   b. 1,790
   c. 2,015
   d. 2,165

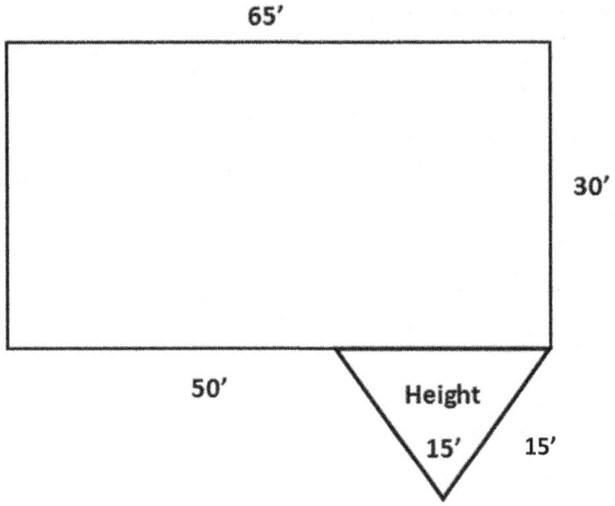

3. Using the diagram above, what is the living area square footage of the home?

   a. 1,612
   b. 1,950
   c. 2,062
   d. 2,175

 © 2019 – 3 Wise Teachers, LLC

POINTS AND YIELD TO THE LENDER

If a borrower wants to lower his interest rate on a loan the lender may add "points" to the borrower's closing costs to be paid at closing. A bank will lower the interest rate charged by 1/8 (0.125) of one percent by charging 1 discount point (1%) to the loan. If the borrower wanted to lower his interest rate from 4.5% to 4.375%, a 1% fee would be charged against the loan amount. For a $100,000 loan, the borrower would be charged a one-time fee of $1,000 (paid at closing). When points are paid the loan may be referred to as a "Buy-down" mortgage.

Discount points are commonly tested as part of comprehensive problem, such as calculating the amount the buyer will need to pay at closing, rather than a stand-alone math problem.

Other questions may ask you to determine the lender yield (actual rate of interest earned) – take the interest rate on the note and add .125% for every point paid by the buyer. If a note carried an interest rate of 5.5% and the buyer paid 2 discount points the yield to the lender would be 5.75% (5.5% + .25%). The yield to the lender would not include origination fees, even though they are paid to the lender.

Loan to value is calculated by taking the loan and dividing by value. You can determine the amount that a lender is willing to lend by multiplying the sales price by the loan to value (LTV).

Example 1. The lender is charging 1.5 points for a $212,000 loan.

Discount Points: 1.5 points = 1.5% of the loan amount
Discount Points Cost: $212,000 X 1.5% = $3,180.

Example 2. Sam is acquiring a loan for $150,000 with an interest rate of 4.5% with 2 discount points and a loan origination fee of 1%. How much will he pay in discount points? What is the yield to the lender? How much will he pay for the loan origination fee?

Discount Points: 2 points = 2% of the loan amount
Discount Point Cost: $150,000 X 2% (or 0.02) = $3,000
Discount Points – Rate Change: 2 X .125% = .25%
Yield to Lender: 4.5% + .25% = 4.75%
Loan Origination: $150,000 X 1% = $1,500

Example 3. David would like to purchase a home with a $340,000 loan for 30 years at 4.25%. The bank initially offered him a loan at 4.75%. How many points would David need to pay to get his desired interest rate? How much would that cost him?

Number of Points: David needs a .50% change in the interest rate. 0.50 ÷ 0.125 = 4 Points
Discount Point Cost: 4% (or .04) X $340,000 = $13,600

Problems for you to Solve (solutions page 85):

1. A buyer is purchasing a home for $300,000 by obtaining a conventional loan for $280,000. The lender is charging 1% origination and 2 discount points. What will the buyer pay to the lender for discount points?

    a. $2,800
    b. $3,000
    c. $5,600
    d. $6,000

2. A buyer is purchasing a home for $250,000 by obtaining a 30-year conventional loan with an 85% LTV. The lender requires the borrower to pay 2% origination and 1.5 discount points. How much will the lender charge for the discount points?

    a. $3,187.50
    b. $3,750.00
    c. $4,250.00
    d. $5,000.00

3. A lender is charging 1% origination and 2 discount points on a 30-year conventional loan of $200,000 with an interest rate of 6%. What is the yield to the lender?

    a. 5.750%
    b. 5.875%
    c. 6.125%
    d. 6.250%

LOAN TO VALUE

The LTV percentage is the comparison of the loan amount to the value of the home. For financing purposes, the bank will determine the value based on the **lower** of the sales price of the home, or the appraised value. How the percentage is calculated is in the name: loan to value = Loan ÷ Value.

Problems will either state that a borrower is purchasing a home with an X% LTV or that the borrower made an X% Down Payment. For Example:

80% LTV = 80% Loan and 20% Down Payment
85% LTV = 85% Loan and 15% Down Payment
10% Down = 90% LTV and 10% Down Payment
 5% Down = 95% LTV and 5% Down Payment

To Calculate the loan Amount:
Sales Price (or appraised value) X Loan to Value

Example 1. Greg is purchasing a home for $124,000 and has been approved for a 95% LTV, how much money will he be borrowing?

$124,000 X 95% (or .95) = $117,800

Example 2. Candace is purchasing a home for $275,250. The appraisal has come back at $269,900. What is the maximum loan she can receive with an 80% LTV? How much is her down payment?

Loan Amount: $269,900 X 80% (or .80) = $215,920
Down Payment: $275,250 - $215,920 = $59,330

FACTORS and PITI PAYMENT

Amortization is paying the total principal and interest of a loan in equal monthly payments. Most monthly payments are made up of 4 components, PITI (Principal, Interest, Taxes and Insurance). For the purpose of this course, we use a mortgage factor to determine the Principal and Interest only, then add the monthly taxes and insurance.

The mortgage factor is a dollar amount paid for every $1,000 of the loan amount. It may be referred to as a factor or state that the loan amortizes at "X".

Factors will be given in a problem and is based upon the interest rate and the length of time the money is borrowed. The calculation will always be for a fixed or level-payment loan.

Sample Amortization Chart

Annual Interest Rate In Percent	Years to Fully Amortize Loan	15 years	20 years	25 years	30 years
7.50		9.27	8.06	7.39	6.99
7.75		9.41	8.21	7.55	7.16
8.00		9.56	8.36	7.72	7.34
8.25		9.70	8.52	7.88	7.51
8.50		**9.85**	**8.68**	**8.05**	**7.69**
8.75		9.99	8.84	8.22	7.57

Look at the left hand column for the annual interest rate (8.5%) look to the right to find the corresponding number for the loan to fully amortize (30 years). Our factor for a 30-year loan at 8.5% annual interest rate is 7.69 (this is not a percent – think of it as $7.69). It represents a dollar amount per month per $1,000 borrowed.

Loan Amount / 1,000 X mortgage factor = Monthly **PI** payment

The monthly taxes and insurance are 1/12 of the annual property tax and hazard insurance bills for the property. **TI**

Total monthly payment = PITI = (Monthly PI + 1/12 Annual Taxes + 1/12 Annual Insurance)

Example 1. What would be the PI payment on a $185,000 loan with a factor of 5.65?

$185,000 / 1,000 X $5.65 = $1,045.25

Example 2. Logan's lender is charging $4.38 per thousand borrowed on his mortgage loan. If his PI payment is $1,180 per month, how much is his loan amount?

$1,180 / $4.38 X 1,000 = $269,406.39

Example 3. What is Jina's PITI payment if she borrowed $305,000 that amortizes at 5.03, property taxes are $4,500 and the hazard insurance costs $1,200 per year?

PI Payment: $305,000 ÷ 1,000 X 5.03 = $1,534.15
Monthly TI: ($4,500 + 1,200) ÷ 12 = $475
PITI Payment: $1,534.15 + $475 = $2,009.15

Problems for you to Solve (solutions page 85):

1. What is the monthly PI on a 240,000 loan at 7.5% interest rate for 30 years? (reference chart above)

2. What would be the total PITI payment for the loan above if annual taxes and insurance were $4500/yr?

3. A What would Tony's PI payment be if he purchased a home for $325,000 with a conventional loan at 95% LTV for 30 years at an 8% interest rate? (reference chart above)

4. What would his total PITI payment be if annual taxes are $5600/yr, insurance is $1200/yr and he has a car payment of $430/mo?

SIMPLE INTEREST

There are multiple ways that you will be tested on interest – calculation of monthly interest on a loan to determine the payment principal, calculation of interim / prepaid interest for closing problems (which will be covered in the proration section), total interest paid over the life of the loan and the amount of interest saved by selecting a lower payment term (ex: 15-year loan vs 30-year loan).

Total Interest Paid over the Life of the Loan

When calculating the total interest paid over the life of the loan, you must know or calculate the monthly principal and interest payment and the term of the loan. You must calculate the total principal and interest payments. When the problem has only one loan, then you would back out the original loan amount (principal). When the problem is comparing two loans, so long as both loans have the same principal borrowed, there is no need to back out principal since they are the same.

Calculate Number of Payments: 30-year term x 12 months/year = 360 months total
Monthly PI Payment X 360 payments = Total Principal and Interest Payments
Total PI Payments – Original Loan Amount = Total Interest Over the Life of the Loan

Example 1. Jackie obtains a $180,000 loan at 5.25% interest rate to be repaid over 30 years with a factor (amortization rate) 4.375. What is the total interest that Jackie will pay?

Monthly PI Payment: $180,000 ÷ 1,000 X 4.375 = $787.50
Total PI Payments: $787.50 X 360 payments = $283,500
Total Interest: $283,500 - $180,000 Loan = $103,500

Example 2. Mark purchases a home for $350,000 requiring a 20% down payment. He is weighing 2 loans; a 30-year loan at 5.75% interest rate with an amortization rate of 5.835 and a 15-year loan at 5.0% interest rate with an amortization rate (factor) of 7.907. How much will Mark save if he selects the 15-year loan rather than the 30-year loan?

Loan Amount: $350,000 X 80% LTV = $280,000
30 Year Monthly PI Payment: $280,000 ÷ 1,000 X 5.835 = $1,633.80
Total PI Payments: $1,633.80 X 360 payments = $588,168

15 Year Monthly PI Payment: $280,000 ÷ 1,000 X 7.907 = $2,213.96
Total PI Payments: $2,213.96 X 180 payments = $398,513

Savings: $588,168 - $398,513 = $189,655

Problems for you to Solve (solutions page 86):

1. Sara is getting a loan for $165,000 with a 4.75% interest rate for 30 years with a factor of 5.22. How much interest will be paid over the life of the loan?

    a. $165,068
    b. $145,068
    c. $130,450
    d. $117,150

2. Alexander is purchasing a property for $114,000 with a 3.5% down payment. The interest rate is 4.375% for 30-years. Property taxes and insurance will cost $110 per month. How much interest will be paid over the life of the loan if it amortizes at 4.9904?

    a. $ 87,626
    b. $ 97,628
    c. $144,388
    d. $197,636

3. Mary is weighing the loan options for a property and wants to know how much she can save by selecting a 15-year loan rather than a 30-year loan, where the loans amortize at 6.135 and 4.288 respectively. In both cases she will borrow $195,000. How much interest will be saved?

   a. $280,170
   b. $180,170
   c. $105,679
   d. $ 85,679

4. A borrower is purchasing a property for $375,000 with a $50,000 down payment. He is deciding between 2 loans with the same original principal balance. The 30-year loan carries an interest rate of 4.75% with a factor of 5.22. The 15-year loan carries an interest rate of 4.25% with a factor of 7.53. How much more will the 30-year loan cost versus the 15-year loan?

   a. $170,235
   b. $196,425
   c. $255,937
   d. $295,312

LOAN AMORTIZATION – Balance After 1 Payment

Amortization occurs when a borrower makes a payment that is comprised of principal and interest. A fixed or level loan will have equal monthly payments. Most monthly payments are made up of 4 components, PITI (Principal, Interest, Taxes and Insurance). When calculating the balance after one payment make sure that you are using the PI portion only as TI goes to an escrow account and will be paid out when taxes and insurance are due. The principal portion of the payment reduces the amount owed and the interest portion is the profit to the lender.

You may be required to calculate the PI payment using a factor (see Factors and PITI Payments above) or it will be provided in the question along with the loan amount and interest rate. We must calculate the monthly interest, subtract it from the total PI payment, in order to calculate the amount of principal paid.

Monthly Interest: Loan X Rate ÷12
Principal Payment: PI Payment – Monthly Interest
New Balance: Loan – Principal Payment

Example 1. What is the loan balance after the first payment if the PI payment is $1,655.85 per month with a loan of $249,000 at 7% interest for 30 years?

Monthly Interest: $249,000 X 7% ÷ 12 = $1,452.50
Principal Payment: PI $1,655.85 – I $1,452.50 = P $203.35
New Balance: $249,000 – $203.35 = $248,796.65

Example 2. James purchased a house for $300,000 by obtaining an 80% LTV mortgage at 5.5% interest for 15-years that amortizes at 8.18. What is the mortgage balance after 1 payment?

Loan Amount: $300,000 X 80% (or .80) = $240,000
Monthly PI Payment: $240,000 ÷ 1,000 X 8.18 = $1,963.20
Monthly Interest: $240,000 X 5.5% ÷ 12 = $1,100
Principal Payment: PI $1,963.20 – I $1,100 = P $863.20
New Balance: $240,000 – $863.20 = $239,136.80

Problems for you to Solve (solutions page 87):

1. Shawn is obtaining a mortgage loan for $175,000 for 30 years. The interest rate is 4.75% with a mortgage factor of 5.22. What is the mortgage balance after his first payment, rounded to the nearest dollar?

    a. $174,087
    b. $174,500
    c. $174,779
    d. $174,909

2. Sophie purchased a property for $188,000 with a 3.5% down payment. The interest rate is 4.375% for 30-years with a factor of 4.9904. Property taxes and insurance will cost $210 per month. What is the mortgage balance after one payment, rounded to the nearest dollar?

    a. $180,515
    b. $181,176
    c. $187,062
    d. $187,747

3. Riley purchased a property for $249,900 with 10% down at 4.5% interest for 30-years and a PITI Payment of $1,340. Property taxes and Insurance total $2,400 annually. What is the mortgage balance after one payment, rounded to the nearest dollar?

    a. $249,697
    b. $248,503
    c. $224,613
    d. $224,413

4. Grace purchased a property for $885,000 with 20% down at 4.75% interest for 30 years amortized at 5.22. Property taxes and insurance for the year are $14,000 and $3,000 respectively. What is the mortgage balance after one payment, rounded to the nearest dollar?

    a. $706,883
    b. $707,107
    c. $883,883
    d. $884,107

QUALIFYING BUYER FOR A CONVENTIONAL LOAN

Your debt-to-income ratio is all your monthly debt payments divided by your gross monthly income. This number is one way lenders measure your ability to manage the payments you make every month to repay the money you have borrowed.

On an exam, it will ask you to calculate two numbers: The Housing Debt and the Total Debt. Housing for a conventional loan usually cannot exceed 28% of your monthly gross income. Recurring Debt is your house payment and any additional recurring payments (i.e., auto payment, credit card payment, mortgage payments). Recurring debt usually cannot exceed 36%. For FHA and VA loans these ratios maybe different. The question will tell you which ratios to use. For example, a 28/36 rule, means that the housing ratio alone is 28%.

To calculate your debt-to-income ratio, <u>add up all monthly debt payments</u> and <u>divide</u> them <u>by</u> your <u>gross monthly income</u>. Gross monthly income is generally the amount of money you have earned before your taxes and other deductions are taken out.

<u>Housing</u>	<u>Total Debt</u>
Principal & Interest	PITI
Taxes & Insurance	Long Term Debt (credit cards, student loan, etc.)

When you are calculating these qualification problems, you will only use recurring debts that are greater than 6 months from being paid off. These types of problems may ask you to calculate maximum loan amount, minimum income required, or maximum monthly debt. The equations for those calculations are below.

Does the Buyer Qualify?

Monthly gross income X 28% = Maximum monthly housing expense

Monthly gross income X 36% = Maximum monthly housing & recurring debt expenses

*Note borrower will need to qualify under both ratios
*The buyer qualifies if the payment equals or is below the maximum housing and total debt.

What is the Minimum Income Needed to Qualify?

Maximum monthly housing expense / 28% = Required monthly gross income

Maximum monthly housing & debt expense / 36% = Required monthly gross income

*Note, the higher of the two calculations will be the one that is the minimum required gross income

*Be careful as the problem could ask for monthly or yearly income.

What is the Maximum Debt a Borrower Can Have and Still Qualify?

Monthly gross income X 36% = Maximum monthly housing & recurring debt expense

Maximum monthly housing & debt expense – Monthly housing = Maximum debt

Example 1. What is the minimum Monthly income need to qualify under the following scenario?

Robin wants to purchase a property that has a monthly PI of $1512 and Taxes and Insurance are $1,800.00 (annual). She has other monthly long term debt of $350 (car loan), $150 (Credit Cards), and $225 (Student Loan). What is the monthly income needed to qualify? [recall that you must use the higher of the two amounts, because you must qualify for both ratios.] We will use the 28/36 qualifying ratios.

Housing Expense
$1,512.00 (PI)
$ 150.00 (TI)

$ 1,662.00 (PITI)

$1,662.00 ÷ 0.28 = $5,936

Total Debt
$350.00 (Car Loan)
$150.00 (Credit Cards)
$225.00 (Student Loan)

$725.00 + **$1,662.00** = $2,387.00
$2,387 ÷ 0.36 = **$6,631.00**

$6,631.00 is the higher amount per month.

Example 2. What is the maximum PITI payment the borrower can have and still qualify for the loan under the following scenario?

A buyer is obtaining a conventional loan that requires 28/36 ratios. He earns $150,000 a year and has a $1,300 monthly revolving debt. What is his maximum PITI payment?

Monthly income: $150,000 ÷ 12 = $12,500
Max Housing: $12,500 X 28% = $3,500
Max Total debt: $12,500 X 36% = $4,500
Max PITI Given Other Debts: $4,500 - $1,300 = $3,200

Maximum PITI is the lower of the two, or $3,200. The buyer needs to qualify under both ratios – Housing

Example 3. Does the borrower qualify for the mortgage based on the scenario below?

A buyer is obtaining a conventional loan and earns $70,000 a year. He currently has long term monthly expenses of $400 for a car loan and $200 for a credit card? The projected monthly PI payment is $1,200 and annual taxes and insurance are $4,800. Will the buyer qualify for the loan?

Monthly Income: $70,000 ÷12 = $5,833
Max Housing: $5,833 X 28% = $1,633
Max Total Debt: $5,833 X 36% = $2,100

Actual Housing: $1,200 + $400 = $1,600 (Buyer Qualifies under Housing)
Actual Total Debt: $1,600 + $600 = $2,200 (Buyer Does Not Qualify under TD)

Problems for you to Solve (solutions page 88):

1. Jim makes $66,000/year. He wants to buy a house with a conventional loan, with a monthly PI payment of $1,200. Taxes and Insurance are $250/mo. He has a car payment of $300/mo and other long-term debt of $350/mo. Does he qualify?

    I. Qualify under Housing Expenses
    II. Qualify under Total Debt

      a. I Only
      b. II Only
      c. Both I and II
      d. Neither I nor II

2. Veronica makes $100,000/year and has long term debt of $520/mo. She is looking at a home whose annual taxes are $2400/year and insurance is $900/year. What is the most that her PITI payment can be if she is getting a conventional loan?

      a. $2,058
      b. $2,333
      c. $2,480
      d. $3,000

3. Polly has a gross annual income of $60,000 and her husband Mike makes $4,500/mo. The projected PI payment is $1,600 with monthly taxes of $400, monthly insurance of $200 and monthly HOA dues of $50. The couple have monthly car payments of $800, student loans of $300 and credit card payments $50. Which of the following statements is correct?

   I. Qualify under Housing Expenses
   II. Qualify under Total Debt

   a. I Only
   b. II Only
   c. Both I and II
   d. Neither I nor II

4. Xavier's bank will give him a loan with a factor of 9.65. If his annual income is $120,000/year and he has debts of $980 per month, and his T&I are estimated at $300/month, what would be the maximum PITI payment under conventional loan ratios of 28% housing and 36% total debt?

   a. $2,500
   b. $2,620
   c. $2,800
   d. $2,920

5. Betty is purchasing a property for $235,000 with a $25,000 down payment for 15 years with an interest rate of 4.125% and a factor of 7.46. Annual taxes, insurance and homeowners dues are $3,500, $900 and $600 respectively. She has a car loan for $330/month, credit card payments of $200/mo and a student loan of $160/month. What is the minimum monthly income she needs to qualify under the conventional loan ratios, rounded to the nearest dollar?

   a. $ 7,083
   b. $ 7,426
   c. $84,996
   d. $89,112

6. A couple with $175,000 annual income wants to purchase a home that has a PI payment of $3,000 per month. Annual taxes, insurance and homeowner dues are $12,000 per year. They have a vehicle loan that costs $300 per month. How much additional long-term debt may the couple have and still qualify for a conventional mortgage?

   a. $ 83
   b. $ 950
   c. $1,250
   d. $1,950

CLOSING THE REAL ESTATE TRANSACTION

PRORATIONS

There are several types of calculations that may be prorated: taxes, rent, interim/prepaid interest and HOA dues. Whatever fee listed above is being prorated, the calculation is as follows. Unless otherwise stated, it is understood that there are 30 days in each month or 360 days in the year (rather than actual days – which would be 365, unless a leap year 366).

Annual fee ÷ 360 = Daily fee amount

Daily fee amount X # of days = prorated fee amount

When it comes to prorations, it is important to understand who is responsible for which portion of an annual bill that will be split between buyer and seller. The proration calculation is a simple one, but understanding whether it is a credit or debit and to the buyer or seller can be a little more challenging.

When performing these calculations, the seller either pays (taxes) or gets paid (rent) for the day of closing. On the national exam, the buyer may be responsible for the day of closing. For the state exam, unless the problem states otherwise, the seller is responsible.

The seller owns the property on day of settlement, regardless of the number of hours. Prorations are made through and including the day of closing. The seller typically pays or is paid through the day of closing. It is important to read the problem carefully since the test may state that the buyer takes responsibility for taxes on the day of closing.

Prorations are either **accrued** (not paid and will be paid at closing) or **pre-paid/interim** (paid before closing). Remember the tax bill comes out on September 1. Usually if the closing is before September 1 they have not been paid. After September 1 they may or may not have been paid. Taxes are paid in the arrears and are due no later than Jan 5 of the following year. [Note: Do not confuse prepaid items in prorations with prepaids required by the lender in the closing statement (escrow of property tax, insurance and mortgage insurance.]

Prepaids required by the lender appear on Other Costs F: Prepaids for;

- Homeowner's Insurance Premium (one year)
- Private Mortgage Insurance or Mortgage Insurance Premium (one year)
- Interim/Prepaid Mortgage Interest from closing date to the end of month (loan x rate ÷ 360 to get $/day times the number of days between closing and end of month)

Interim / Prepaid Interest

This type of interest is paid by the buyer for their new loan to cover the day of closing through the end of the month. Mortgage interest is paid in arrears – for example a closing that is held on April 7th, no payment is made in May and the first payment will be due June 1. June 1's payment is for May's interest. Therefore the buyer is responsible for paying the interest for the remainder of the month which is paid at closing. This is the one instance where the buyer is responsible for the day of closing, as the seller has no responsibility for the buyer's loan costs.

Loan Amount X Interest rate = Annual Interest; Annual Interest / 360 = Daily Interest; Daily Interest X # of days left in month (including closing day) = Interim Interest due

Example 1. Nancy is buying a home for $143,000 with a 10% down payment at a 4.5% interest rate. Closing is set for April 7th. What is Nancy's interim interest?

Loan Amount: $143,000 X 90% = $128,700
Daily Interest: $128,700 X 4.5% ÷ 360 = $16.0875
Number of Days: 30 – 7 + 1 = 24 Days
Interim Interest: $16.0875 X 24 = $386.10

Example 2. Brian is borrowing $225,000 at 4.875% interest. Closing is set for Sep. 20th. What is his interim interest?

Daily Interest: $225,000 X 4.875% ÷ 360 = $30.4688
Number of Days: 30 – 20 + 1 = 11 Days
Interim Interest: $30.4688 X 11 = $335.16

Example 3. Leigh Ann is purchasing a house for $425,000 with a conventional loan with 10% down. The interest rate is 4.25% with a factor of 4.92. What is the interim interest charge if the closing date is June 18th?

Daily Interest: $425,000 X 90% = $382,500 X 4.25% = $16,256.25 ÷ 360 = $45.1562
Number of Days: 30 – 18 + 1 = 13 Days
Interim Interest: $45.1562 X 13 Days = $587.03

Example 4. Becky is purchasing a house for $180,000 with a conventional loan with 5% down. The interest rate is 5.5% with a factor of 5.68. What is the interim interest charge if the closing date is Aug 27th?

Daily Interest: $180,000 X 95% = $171,000 X 5.5% = $9,405 ÷ 360 = $26.125
Number of Days: 30 – 27 + 1 = 4 Days
$26.125/day x 4 days = $104.50

Problems for you to Solve (solutions page 90):

1. Shaneka is buying her first home, with a loan of 192,000 at a 5.5% interest rate. Her closing is 3/25. What is her interim interest?

    a. $117.34
    b. $146.67
    c. $176.00
    d. $205.33

2. Carlos is buying a home for $315,000. He is getting a conventional loan at 5% interest and putting 10% down. His closing is November 10th. What is his interim interest?

    a. $866.26
    b. $850.00
    c. $826.88
    d. $787.50

Accrued Interest

In the rare case where there is a loan assumption question, you may be required to calculate accrued interest. Generally, the seller will pay the buyer his/her portion of the interest and the buyer will pay the mortgage on the next due date.

The entry is debit to the seller and credit to the buyer, because the buyer is taking over the loan (assuming it).

Example 1. A buyer is closing on a property on June 18 by assuming the seller's mortgage. The loan has a balance on June 1 of $285,491 and carries an interest rate of 4%. What is the entry on the closing disclosure?

Daily Rate: $285,491 X 4% ÷ 360 = $31.7212
Charge to Seller: 18 Days X $31.7212 = $570.98
Debit Seller / Credit Buyer – Buyer Pays Mortgage on July 1

Example 2. A buyer is closing on a property on September 12 by assuming the seller's mortgage. The loan has a balance on September 1 of $188,286 and carries an interest rate of 5.5%. What is the entry on the closing disclosure?

Daily Rate: $188,286 X 5.5% ÷ 360 = $28.7659
Charge to Seller: 12 Days X $28.7659 = $345.19
Debit Seller / Credit Buyer – Buyer Pays Mortgage on October 1

Property Taxes – North Carolina

For property taxes, there are 3 possible scenarios that could result in 3 different determinations of who is credited or debited. Put yourself in the place of the buyer or seller to help determine the correct entry. You would not want to be the seller and have to pay the full year of taxes when the closing takes place during the year. You would not want to be the buyer and be held responsible for the property taxes during the time that the seller owns the property.

1 – For closings that take place prior to 9/1 in any year, the buyer will pay the tax bill after the closing, (the seller has not yet paid the bill b/c it is not yet due). So the tax proration will be a debit to the seller and the same amount will be credited to the buyer at the closing.

2 – For closings on or after 9/1, if the seller has already paid the property tax bill. The prorated amount will be the portion that the buyer is responsible for will be debited from the buyer and credited to the seller.

3 – For closings on or after 9/1 for which the seller has not paid the property tax bill, the buyer and seller will each have a different amount of tax that they are responsible for, and each will be debited their own amount on the settlement statement.

Recall: Property taxes in North Carolina are calculated as follows.

Assessed Value / 100 X Tax Rate

Example 1: Taxes Not Yet Paid [ACCRUED], based upon previous years tax bill

If closing is on April 11th, The seller is responsible for the period from January 1 through and including April 11. The annual property tax bill is $1,980 and unpaid.

Seller Number of days: Jan 30 + Feb 30 + Mar 30 + Apr 11 = 101 days.
Daily Rate Tax: $1980 ÷ 360 = $5.50/day
Seller Charge: 101 days x $5.50 = $555.50

The seller owes the buyer $555.50. The entry will appear a debit to the seller, credit to the buyer, because the buyer will pay the entire tax bill at the end of the year.

Example 2: Taxes Paid – Buyer to Reimburse Seller

When taxes are paid by the seller we are seeking to determine how much the buyer will need to reimburse the seller. I recommend calculating the buyer's number of days rather than the seller number of days as the seller amount will be used as a distractor.

What is the entry if closing is on October 18, taxes are $1,980 and have been paid by the seller?

Buyer Number of days: Oct (30-18=12) + Nov 30 + Dec 30 = 72 days.
Daily Rate Tax: $1980 ÷ 360 = $5.50/day
Buyer Charge: 72 days x $5.50 = $396.00

In this case, since the taxes have been paid by the seller for the year, the buyer owes the seller $396.00. It would appear as a debit to the buyer, a credit to the seller.

Example 3: Taxes Not Yet Paid (to be paid at Closing by the attorney).

What is the entry if closing is set for October 20, taxes are $1,980 for the year and have not been paid by seller?

Use the double debit method, where the attorney will pay the tax bill when the deed is recorded.

Buyer Number of days: Oct (30 – 20 = 10) + Nov 30 + Dec 30 = 70 days.
Daily Rate Tax: $1980 ÷ 360 = $5.50/day
Buyer Charge: 70 days x $5.50 = $385.00
Seller Charge: $1,980 - $385 = $1,595.00

In this case, since the taxes have not been paid and the problem states that the attorney will pay the bill, debit the buyer $385.00 and debit the seller $1,595.00.

Problems for you to Solve (solutions page 91):

1. Closing is set for 10/6. Taxes are $2,900 for the year and are unpaid by the seller. What is the prorated tax charge and to whom is it a credit or debit?

    a. Seller debit $2,223.33 / Buyer debit $ 676.67
    b. Seller debit $ 676.67 / Buyer debit $2,223.33
    c. Seller debit $ 676.67 / Buyer credit $ 676.67
    d. Seller debit $2,223.33 / Buyer credit $2,223.33

2. Closing is set for 3/14. Taxes are $4,500 for the year and are unpaid. What is the prorated tax charge, and to whom is it a credit or debit?

    a. Seller credit $3,575 / Buyer debit $3,575
    b. Seller debit $3,575 / Buyer credit $3,575
    c. Seller credit $ 925 / Buyer debit $ 925
    d. Seller debit $ 925 / Buyer credit $ 925

3. Closing is set for 11/17. Taxes are $3,300 for the year and have already been paid by the seller. What is the prorated tax charge, and to whom is it a credit or debit?

    a. Seller credit $2,905.83 / Buyer debit $2,905.83
    b. Seller debit $2,905.83 / Buyer credit $2,905.83
    c. Seller credit $ 394.17 / Buyer debit $ 394.17
    d. Seller debit $ 394.17 / Buyer credit $ 394.17

4. A property recently sold for $289,000 with an assessed value of $240,000 located in Alamance County, NC. The closing is scheduled for September 21st. What is the tax proration if the tax rate is $1.50 and have not been paid by the seller?

   a. Seller debit $2,610.00 / Buyer debit $ 990.00
   b. Seller debit $3,142.87 / Buyer debit $1,192.13
   c. Seller debit $ 990.00 / Buyer credit $ 990.00
   d. Seller debit $1,192.13 / Buyer credit $1,192.13

5. A property has a fair market value of $1,200,000 with an assessed value of $960,000 that is located in Durham County, NC. The county tax rate is $0.75 and city tax rate is $0.50. The property is sold on February 9th and taxes have not been paid by the seller. What is the property tax proration if the property is located in the county and taxes are unpaid?

   a. Seller debit $ 780 / Buyer debit $6,420
   b. Seller debit $ 780 / Buyer credit $ 780
   c. Seller debit $ 975 / Buyer debit $8,025
   d. Seller debit $ 975 / Buyer credit $ 975

6. A property sold for $480,000 on December 21st, with the seller paying the bill for the entire year. The assessed value is 90% of the sales price. What is the tax entry if the property tax rate is $1.25?

   a. Seller debit $5,265 / Buyer debit $ 135
   b. Seller debit $5,820 / Buyer debit $ 150
   c. Seller credit $ 135 / Buyer debit $ 135
   d. Seller debit $ 150 / Buyer credit $ 150

Property Tax – National

Recall that property taxes are calculated for the National portion of the exam as follows:

AV / 1,000 X Mills Rate

Property taxes are typically paid by the seller through the day of closing. For testing purposes, you may be required to add or subtract a day when the buyer agrees to be responsible for the day of closing. When closing is before 9/1 and taxes are unpaid, you would calculate the seller number of days and therefore subtract a day.

When closing is after 9/1 you would calculate the buyer number of days and therefore add a day.

National Question (Taxes Not Paid): [Ask yourself: "Who is paying? When?"]

Monica is purchasing a property for $280,000 with an assessed value of 85%. The tax rate is 14 mills, closing on April 17th. What is the tax proration entry <u>if the buyer pays the day of closing</u>? (read carefully)

$280,000 X 85% = $238,000 / 1,000 = 238 X 14 = $3,332
$3,332 / 360 = $9.2555
JFM (90) + A 16 = 106 Days
$9.2555 X 106 = $981.09
Db. Seller / Cr. Buyer $981.09

National Question (Taxes Have Been Paid by Seller):

Rachel is purchasing a property for $860,000 with an assessed value of 80%. The tax rate is 11 mills, closing on Oct 26th. What is the tax proration entry if taxes have been paid by the seller and <u>the buyer will pay the day of closing</u>? (read question very carefully)

Oct – 30 – 26 = 4 + 1 = 5 Days
O 5 + ND 60 = 65 Days
$860,000 X 80% = $688,000 / 1000 = 688 X 11 = $7,568 ÷ 360 = $21.0222
$21.0222 X 65 days = $1,366.44
Db Buyer / Cr Seller = $1,366.44

National Question (Taxes Not Paid by Seller):

Corey is purchasing a property for $550,000 with an assessed value of 95%. The tax rate is 13 mills, closing on Sept 3rd. What is the tax proration entry if taxes have not been paid by the seller and <u>the buyer will pay the day of closing</u>? (read very carefully)

30 – 3 = 27 + 1 = 28 days
S 28 + OND 90 = 118 Days
$550,000 X 95% = $522,500 / 1000 = $522.5 X 13 mills = $6,792.50 ÷ 360 = $18.8680
$18.8680 X 118 = Buyer $2,226.43
$6,792.50 - $2,226.43 = Seller $4,566.07

Rent Proration

Rents are usually quoted as a monthly amount and may be listed as paid or unpaid. For testing purposes, unless otherwise stated, there are 30 days in the month.

- It is customary for the seller to receive rents for the day of closing and to pay all expenses for that day.
- If any rents for the current month are uncollected when the sale is closed, the buyer often will agree to collect the rents and remit prorated share to the seller.
- If the seller is holding a tenant security deposit, it can be transferred to the buyer by a double-entry (debit seller, credit buyer).
- The tenant's <u>security deposit is not prorated</u>, because it is the tenant's money…not the seller's.
- Be careful about the number of units that are rented and how rent is quoted. Duplex = 2 units, Triplex = 3 units, Quadplex = 4 units

Example 1: What is the entry on the closing disclosure for the following problem?

Assume the monthly rent is $600, settlement takes place on June 21, and the Seller has received the rent for the month of June (Paid in advance).

$600 monthly rent ÷ 30 days = $20/day
21 days (property owned by the seller) x $20/day = $420 seller's share
$600 - $420 = $180 to buyer: Debit seller; credit buyer

Example 2: What is the entry on the closing disclosure for the following problem?

The monthly rent is $675, settlement is June 5, and the seller has not collected rent prior to settlement. The buyer will collect the entire month's rent of $675.

$675 ÷ 30 days = $22.50 per day
5 days (owned by seller) x $22.50 = $112.50 seller's share
Debit buyer; credit seller

Example 3: What is the entry on the closing disclosure for the following problem?

A duplex rents for $1,900 per unit and rent has been collected prior to settlement. Closing is scheduled for December 8.

$1,900 X 2 units ÷ 30 days = $126.6667 per day
Buyer days: 30 – 8 = 22
Entry: Debit Seller / Credit Buyer $126.6667 X 22 = $2,786.67

Problems for you to Solve (solutions page 92):

1. A buyer is purchasing a duplex that rents for $2,500 per unit. Rent is due on first of the month and the tenant paid the rent to the seller on June 5th. Settlement is scheduled for June 25th. What is the entry on the Closing Disclosure?

    a. Seller debit $2,083.33 / Buyer credit $ 416.67
    b. Seller debit $ 416.67 / Buyer debit $2,083.33
    c. Seller debit $ 416.67 / Buyer credit $ 416.67
    d. Seller debit $ 833.33 / Buyer credit $ 833.33

2. A buyer is purchasing a triplex that rents for $1,200 per unit. Rent is due on the first of the month however has not been paid. What is the entry on the Closing Disclosure if settlement is scheduled for April 3rd ?

    a. Seller credit $1,080 / Buyer debit $1,080
    b. Seller debit $3,240 / Buyer credit $3,240
    c. Seller credit $ 360 / Buyer debit $ 360
    d. Seller debit $ 120 / Buyer credit $ 120

3. A buyer is purchasing a duplex that rents for $1,100 per unit. Rent has been paid by both tenants. Settlement is scheduled for December 11th. What is the entry on the Closing Disclosure?

    a. Seller credit $1,393.33 / Buyer debit $1,393.33
    b. Seller debit $1,393.33 / Buyer credit $1,393.33
    c. Seller credit $ 696.67 / Buyer debit $ 696.67
    d. Seller debit $ 696.67 / Buyer credit $ 696.67

HOA Dues Proration

HOA dues may be prorated on a yearly, quarterly or monthly basis. Make sure that you read the problem carefully so that you know how to proceed. The problem should also indicate the party that will be responsible for payment. The proration is very similar to how we calculate tax proration.

    First: Calculate a Daily Rate
    Yearly: Annual Dues ÷ 360
    Quarterly: Quarterly Dues ÷ 90
    Monthly: Monthly Dues ÷ 30

Calculate the number of days depending on if the dues have been paid by the seller, if the dues will be paid by the buyer or if the dues will be paid by the attorney.

Example 1: A buyer purchased a property on May 23rd for $220,000. HOA dues are $150 per month and have been paid for the year by the seller. What would the adjustment be if the seller pays the day of closing?

$150 X 12 = $1,800 ÷ 360 = $5
JFMA 120 + M 23 = 143 Days Seller
$5 X 143 = $715 Seller
$1,800 – 715 = $1,085, Debit Buyer / Credit Seller

Example 2: A buyer purchased a property on Feb 10th for $890,000. HOA dues are $500 per quarter and have not been paid by the seller. What would the adjustment be if the seller pays the day of closing and the attorney will charge each party their respective amounts and pay the quarterly bill at closing?

$500 / 90 = $5.5555
J 30 + F 10 = 40 days Seller
$5.5555 X 40 = $222.22 Seller
$500 – 222.22 = $277.78 Buyer
Double Debit Entry

Problems for you to Solve (solutions page 93):

1. A buyer is purchasing a property that is subject to a homeowner association. The association charges $800 per year to maintain common amenities. The seller has paid for the entire year. What is the entry on the Closing Disclosure if settlement is October 30th?

    a. Seller debit $133.33 / Buyer credit $133.33
    b. Seller credit $133.33 / Buyer debit $133.33
    c. Seller debit $666.67 / Buyer credit $666.67
    d. Seller credit $666.67 / Buyer debit $666.67

2. A buyer is purchasing property that is subject to a quarterly HOA due of $300. The seller has not paid the due and the closing attorney will charge both parties and pay the quarterly bill. What is the entry on the Closing Disclosure if settlement is scheduled for March 18th?

    a. Seller debit $ 40 / Buyer debit $260
    b. Seller debit $260 / Buyer debit $ 40
    c. Seller credit $ 40 / Buyer debit $ 40
    d. Seller debit $260 / Buyer credit $260

3. A buyer is purchasing a property that is subject to a monthly HOA due of $150. The seller has paid the bill for the month. What is the entry on the Closing Disclosure if settlement is scheduled for September 23rd?

    a. Seller credit $115 / Buyer debit $115
    b. Seller debit $ 35 / Buyer credit $ 35
    c. Seller credit $ 35 / Buyer debit $ 35
    d. Seller debit $115 / Buyer credit $115

MINI CLOSING PROBLEM

All of the proration problems lead into one of the toughest questions on the exam, the mini-closing problem. The questions will ask what the seller will net from the sale of the property or what a buyer will need to pay at closing.

You often will be required to calculate interim/prepaid interest and prorate taxes. You will need to know what expenses are typically paid by the buyer or seller. One way to help remember – the seller typically pays C,D and E – commission, deed preparation and excise tax. Other seller expense will depend on the problem, such as courier fees for loan payoff or mortgage satisfaction. The remaining expenses, unless otherwise stated are borne by the buyer – loan origination, discount points, interim/prepaid interest, inspections, etc.

Items that were paid at the time of mortgage application or paid outside closing should be ignored. The problem is asking what the buyer needs to bring to closing not total amount of settlement charges that have been paid.

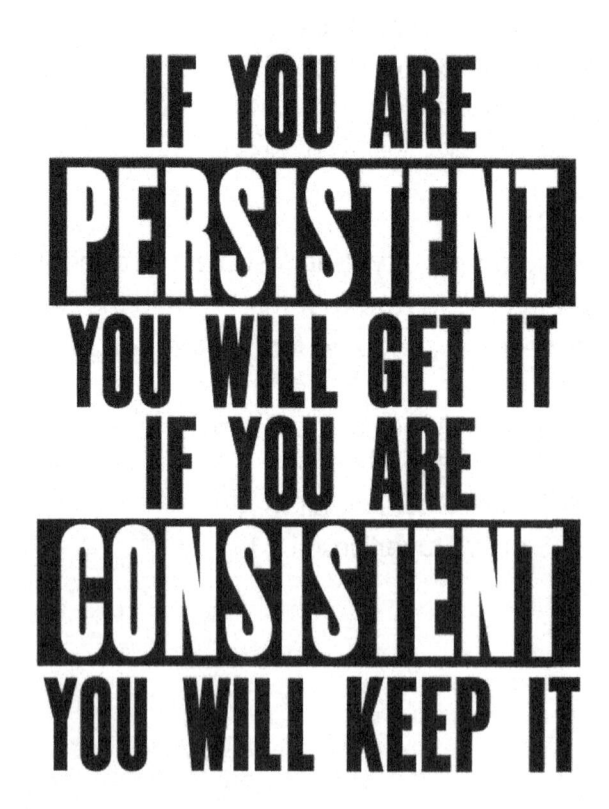

IF YOU ARE PERSISTENT YOU WILL GET IT IF YOU ARE CONSISTENT YOU WILL KEEP IT

Example 1: A buyer purchased a home for $249,650. At the time of the loan application, the buyer also paid $450 for the appraisal and $28 for the credit report fee. The buyer obtained a 30-yr fixed loan for $212,000 at an interest rate of 6.5%, and closed the transaction on November 23rd. The buyer was charged a 3/4 percent loan origination fee and 1 loan discount point. The buyer paid $840 MIP. $2,471 annual property tax on the home was paid by the seller. The $684 annual hazard insurance premium for the first year was paid outside of settlement. At settlement, the lender collected interim interest on the buyer's loan and loan escrow account deposits for 4 months' property taxes plus 2 months each of hazard insurance and mortgage insurance premiums. Based on these facts, how much money (rounded to the nearest dollar) did the buyer have to bring to settlement?

Example 1 Calculation:

Purchase Price	$249,650.00
Less: Loan	-212,000.00
Add: Origination	+1,590.00 ($212,000 x .0075 = $1,590)
Add: Discount Point	+2,120.00 ($212,000 x .01 = $2,120
Add: MIP	+840.00
Add: Tax Proration	+253.96 (see below)
Add: Interim Interest	+306.22 (see below)
Add: Property Tax Escrow	+823.67 ($2371 ÷ 12 = $205.9167 x 4 = $823.67)
Add: Hazard Insurance Escrow	+114.00 ($684 x 12 = $57 x 2 = $114)
Add: Mortgage Insurance Esc	+140.00 ($840 ÷ 12 = $70 x 2 = $140)
Buyer Needed To Close	**$43,837.85**

The appraisal, credit report and annual insurance were paid outside closing – so ignore those expense.

Property Tax Proration:
Since closing is after 9/1 and taxes have been paid, the buyer needs to reimburse the seller – so the entry is debit buyer / credit seller, so we will add this amount above.
Buyer Days: N (7) + D (30) = 37 Days
Daily Rate: $2,471 ÷ 360 = $6.8639
Buyer Taxes: $6.8639 X 37 = $253.96

Interim Interest Calculation:
Days: Nov 23-30 = 7 + 1 = 8 days
Daily Rate: 212,000 x 6.5% = $13,780 ÷ 360 = $38.2778/day
Entry: $38.2778/day x 8 days = $306.22

Example 2: A buyer agrees to purchase a sellers home for $177,350 with closing occurring on October 24, 2016. The buyer paid a $500 earnest money deposit and $250 due diligence fee. The seller agree to pay 5% commission to the brokerage for selling the home. The seller's loan payoff as of closing is $131,490. Property taxes of $1,258 are unpaid as of settlement, and will be paid by the closing attorney using the double debit method. The following expenses were paid by the customary party: Deed preparation $75, deed recording fee $10, excise tax based on North Carolina standard, survey $350 and courier fee for seller's loan payoff of $15. How much did the seller net from the sale of the property?

Example 2 Calculation:

Purchase Price	$177,350.00
Less: Due Diligence	-250.00
Less: Commission	-8,867.50 ($177,350 x .05 = $8,867.50)
Less: Loan Payoff	-131,490.00
Less: Tax Proration	-1,027.37
Less: Deed Prep	-75.00
Less: Excise Tax	-355.00 ($177,350 ÷ 500, round up)
Less: Courier Fee	-15.00
Seller's Net	$35,270.13

The earnest money deposit, deed recording fee and survey are buyer expenses – so ignore them.

Property Tax Proration:
Since closing is after 9/1 and taxes are unpaid, the double debit method is used.
Seller Days: JFMAMJJAS (270) + O (24) = 294 Days
Daily Rate: $1,258 ÷ 360 = $3.4944
Seller Taxes: $3.4944 X 294 = $1,027.37

Problems for you to Solve (solutions page 94):

1. A buyer agrees to purchase a home for $200,000, closing on November 15th with a 95% loan and a 1% origination fee. The closing has the following expenses, paid by the customary party – 5.5% commission, $700 in closing attorney fees, $250 in title insurance, $150 deed preparation, and standard excise tax. Seller payoff of existing mortgage of $77,000. Real estate taxes of $2,400 have been paid. How much will the seller net?

   a. $109,000
   b. $110,800
   c. $111,050
   d. $111,750

2. The selling price of a property is $96,000. This can be financed if the buyer can put down 10% and pay a loan origination fee of 1.5%. The loan is for 30 years with an interest rate of 7.5%, with the buyer responsible for interim interest at closing. The seller has agreed to pay 6% commission on the sale, deed prep of $150 and excise tax according to North Carolina Standards. The buyer paid $1,000 for an earnest money deposit and $500 due diligence fee. How much cash must the buyer bring to complete the transaction, if closing is held January 18th?

   a. $9,612
   b. $9,630
   c. $9,762
   d. $9,780

3. A buyer is purchasing a home for $285,000 with 3.5% down payment and a loan at 3.75% interest per year. Closing is scheduled for October 14th. The following expenses were incurred and paid by the appropriate party: Interim Interest, Deed Prep $150, Survey $400, Excise Tax, 1% Origination, 2 Discount Points, Appraisal $350, Property Tax (unpaid) $2,500. What is the buyer's net due at closing?

   a. $272,220
   b. $293,590
   c. $ 19,990
   d. $ 6,828

4. A owner of a property is selling his home for $369,000 with the closing scheduled for July 30th. The closing has the following expenses paid by the customary party:

   * Loan Origination 1%   * Attorney Closing Fee $900
   * Commission 6%   * Deed Preparation $250
   * Excise Tax $1 per $500   * Seller Mortgage Payoff $135,950
   *Real Estate Tax $4,200, unpaid

   How much will the seller net from closing?

   a. $206,572
   b. $207,472
   c. $208,172
   d. $208,210

5. A buyer is purchasing a home for $265,000 with a 30-year conventional loan that requires a 10% down payment, with an interest rate of 5.5%. The buyer agreed to pay a 1% origination fee. The buyer paid $1,000 due diligence fee and $2,500 earnest money deposit on the effective date of contract. The following expenses will be paid by the customary party:

   * Interim Interest   * Commission 6%
   * Deed Preparation $200   * Excise Tax at $1 per $500

   How much will the buyer need to bring to closing in certified funds if the closing is held on March 15th?

   a. $20,933
   b. $23,583
   c. $25,932
   d. $25,968

VALUATION – SALES COMPARISON APPROACH

When performing CMA calculations to determine probable sales price or range (never 'value' this is performed by licensed appraisers only) you will need to remember the following rules:

a. Adjustments are made to the comparable properties only, <u>never</u> the subject property
b. If the Comp has Superior or better features than the subject property <u>subtract</u> (from comp)
c. If the Comp has Inferior or worse features than the subject property <u>increase or add</u> (to comp)
d. You may have to make an adjustment for appreciation
   Comp Sales price X Appreciation ÷ 12 X # of months = Appreciation adjustment

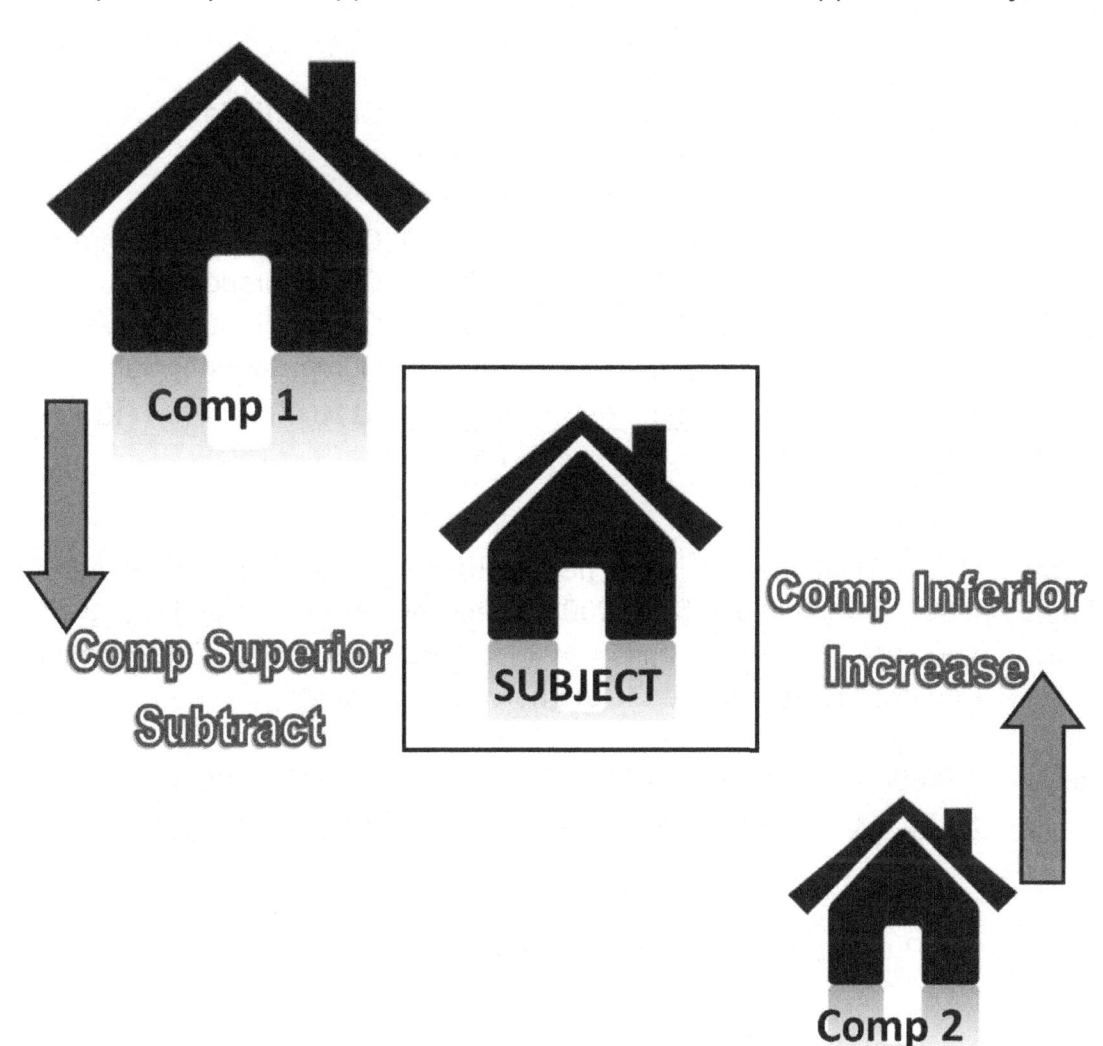

When solving these types of problems, you may place more weight on the value of homes that are closest to the subject property, and you might be asked to calculate a range of values. Often the adjustments are provided in the problem for square footage and other amenities. Some problems will require you to compare the comparable properties to calculate the square footage adjustment or adjustment for one amenity (deck, bathroom, fireplace, etc.).

Example 1. The subject property has 2,400 sqft, 3 bedrooms, 2 baths, a fireplace and a 2 car garage. The comparable property sold 3 months ago for $170,000 and has 2350 sqft, 3 bedrooms, 2.5 baths, no fireplace and a 1 car garage. A half bath typically adds $2,000, fireplaces $2,500, 2 car garage $15,000 and 1 car garage $10,000. The price per sqft of similar properties is $115 and annual appreciation for the area is 4%. What is the adjusted probable selling price rounded to the nearest dollar?

Subject	Comp -	$170,000
2,400 sqft.	2,350 sqft.	+ 5,750 (Comp Inferior Increase)
3 BR	3 BR	No ADJ
2 BA	2 BA	No ADJ
No half BA	1 half BA	- 2,000 (Comp Superior Subtract)
FP	NO FP	+ 2,500 (Comp Inferior Increase)
2 Car Gar	No 2 Car Gar	+ 15,000 (Comp Inferior Increase)
No 1 Car Gar	1 Car Gar	- 10,000 (Comp Superior Subract)
	Apprec	+ 1,700 ($170,000 X 4% ÷ 12 X 3)
Adjusted Comp Probable SP		$182,950

Example 2. The subject property is in a neighborhood with 3 comparables (A,B,C) that sold for $140,000, $125,000 and $160,000 respectively. Comps A and C had superior features of 5,000 and 15,000. Comp B had inferior features of $10,000. What is the probable selling price range rounded to the nearest thousand?

Comp A - $140,000	Comp B - $125,000	Comp C - $160,000
Sup Subtract - $5,000	Inf Increase + $10,000	Sup Subtract - $15,000
$135,000	$135,000	$145,000

Probable Sales Price Range $135,000 - $145,000

Example 3.

Subject	Comp 1 - $145,000	Comp 2 - $135,000	Comp 3 - $140,000
3 BR	3BR	3BR	3BR
1,100	1,200	1,150	1,150
FP	FP	No FP	FP

An appraiser is trying to calculate the market value of a property based on the following 3 comparables. What is the indicated value given the information provided above?

Since the problem does not provide the adjustment for square footage or the value of a fireplace, we will need to determine them by looking at the comps. Comp 1 and Comp 3 are similar except for square footage - $5,000 and 50 sqft, so the value per square foot is $100. Comp 2 and Comp 3 are similar except for the fireplace – the difference in sales price is $5,000 so that is the value of the fireplace.

Now make the adjustments as follows:
Comp 1 - $145,000 - $10,000 sqft = $135,000
Comp 2 - $135,000 - $5,000 sqft + $5,000 FP = $135,000
Comp 3 - $140,000 - $5,000 sqft = $135,000

Problems for you to Solve (solutions page 97):

1. A broker is calculating the probable sales price of a property that is listed for $250,000 which his buyer client wants to make an offer. One comparable property sold 4 months ago for $245,000. The area has seen an annual appreciate rate of 5%. What is the appreciation adjustment the broker would make, rounded to the nearest dollar?

    a. Add $4,083 to the subject property.
    b. Add $4,083 to the comparable property.
    c. Add $4,167 to the subject property.
    d. Add $4,167 to the comparable property.

2. An appraiser has determined that a commercial road frontage in an area where the subject property is located is worth $9,000 per front foot. The subject property lot dimensions are 200' X 1,200'. What is the estimated market value of the property?

   a. $10.8 Million
   b. $ 5.4 Million
   c. $ 3.6 Million
   d. $ 1.8 Million

3. An appraiser has determined that square footage is worth $145 per square foot. She determined that the subject property is inferior by 200 square feet. Which of the following adjustments would the appraiser make?

   a. Subtract $29,000 from the comparable
   b. Add $29,000 to the comparable
   c. Subtract $29,000 from the subject
   d. Add $29,000 to the subject

4. A broker is calculating the probable sales price of a home that she is looking to list. The subject property has 3,400 square feet, 4 bedrooms, 2.5 baths and a deck. The comparable property that sold for $400,000 has 3,200 square feet, 4 bedrooms, 3 baths and a deck. The broker has determined that square footage is worth $100 per square foot, a ½ bath is worth $1,500 and a full bath is worth $2,800. What is the probable sales price indicated by this comparable?

   a. $421,500
   b. $420,000
   c. $418,700
   d. $381,300

5. An appraiser is trying to determine the market value of a property. Based on the following, what is the indicated value?

Subject	Comp 1 - $250,000	Comp 2 - $265,000	Comp 3 - $245,000
2,200 sqft	2,100 sqft	2,300 sqft	2,100 sqft
3 BR	3 BR	3 BR	3 BR
2 BA	2 BA	2 BA	2 BA
FP	FP	No FP	No FP

a. $240,000
b. $253,000
c. $255,000
d. $260,000

6. A property is listed for $185,000. The buyer's agent finds three comps, A B and C that recently sold for $190,000, $187,000 and $195,000 respectively. Comp A had positive features of $7,000, Comp B had negative features of $5,000 and Comp C had positive features of $8,000. What is the indicated range of value?

a. $187,200 - $189,000
b. $183,000 - $192,000
c. $182,000 - $197,000
d. $182,000 - $203,000

7. A buyer is making an offer on a property that is listed for $180,000 that has 1,800 square feet, 3 bedrooms, 2.5 baths and a deck. The agent found a comp that is the most similar that was listed for $190,000 that has 1,750 square feet, 3 bedrooms, 3 baths and no deck. The home sold for $175,000 5 months ago and the market has experience 4% appreciation. The agent has determined that square footage is approximately worth $85/sqft, half bath $1,700, full bath $4,000 and deck $3,500. What is the probable sales price indicated, rounded to the nearest hundred?

a. $172,500
b. $180,500
c. $183,400
d. $198,600

VALUATION – COST APPROACH

This approach to value is used by determining how much it would cost to rebuild the structure new, depreciating it to the current age of the subject property, and then adding the value of the land and improvements. The straight line depreciation method is most often used, which is a constant decrease in value over a period of time.

Depreciation is only taken on the structure, not the land. The value of the land is determined by the sales comparison approach. For the structure, if you are given both actual age and effective age, use the effective age to determine depreciation. Actual age is often a distractor.

The quick formula to memorize is: New – Depreciation + land + Improvements. The detailed calculation is as follows:

Cost of New Improvement: SQFT X Cost/sqft
Annual Straigt-line Depreciation: Cost of New Improvement / Economic Life
Total Depreciation: Annual Depreciation X # of Years of Depreciation

Depreciated Improvement Value: Cost of New Improvement – Total Depreciation
Adjusted Value: Depreciated Improvement Value + Land value

Example 1. An appraiser is valuing a warehouse that is 12,000 sqft with $35,000 in site upgrades. The property is 18 years old. The economic life of the building is 60 years and the effective age of the building is 15 years. The cost to build new is $115 per sqft. A similar lot recently sold for $95,000 without the additional site improvements. What is the value of the property rounded to the nearest hundred dollars?

Building New: 12,000 X $115 = $1,380,000
Depreciation: $1,380,000 ÷ 60 year Useful X 15 year effective = $345,000
Value: $1,380,000 - $345,000 Depr + $95,000 Land + $35,000 Impr = $1,165,000

Example 2. An appraiser is valuing a property that is 7,500 sqft with $12,000 in site upgrades. The economic life of the building is 50 years, actual age of 10 years and the effective age of the building is 5 years. The cost to build new is $240 per sqft. A similar lot recently sold for $120,000 without the additional site improvements. What is the value of the property rounded to the nearest thousand dollars?

Building New: 7,500 X $240 = $1,800,000
Depreciation: $1,800,000 ÷ 50 year Useful X 5 year effective = $180,000
Value: $1,800,000 - $180,000 Depr + $120,000 Land + $12,000 Impr = $1,752,000

Problems for you to Solve (solutions page 98):

1. A real estate broker is valuing a property using the cost approach. The building is 5,000 square feet and the cost to build new has been determined at $195 per square foot. The building has a useful life of 100 years and an effective age of 20 years. What is the yearly straight-line depreciation?

    a. $975,000
    b. $780,000
    c. $195,000
    d. $ 9,750

2. An appraiser is using the cost approach to value a 25 year old building and has determined that the cost to build new is $2,500,000. The useful life of the property is 75 years and the effective age is 15 years. What is the indicated amount of depreciation, rounded to the nearest thousand?

    a. $ 500,000
    b. $ 833,000
    c. $1,500,000
    d. $1,667,000

3. A broker is using the cost approach to determine the probable sales price of a property that has 15,000 square feet. The cost to build new is $175 per square foot. The building has a useful life of 80 years and an effective age of 20 years. The land and improvements are valued at $75,000. What is the indicated probable sales price?

    a. $ 656,000
    b. $ 731,000
    c. $2,044,000
    d. $2,625,000

4. An appraiser is trying to determine the value of a property using the cost approach. The building is 4,000 square feet and is 20 years old. The useful life of the building is 200 years with an effective age of 15 years. The value of the land using the sales comparison approach is $60,000 without accounting for $30,000 in improvements. What is the property worth if the cost to build new is $150 per square foot?

   a. $555,000
   b. $615,000
   c. $645,000
   d. $690,000

5. A buyer is interested in purchasing a school building that has 25,000 square feet, is 25 years old with a useful life of 155 years. The cost to build new is $145 per square foot. The broker, using the sales comparison approach determined the probable sales price of the land at $200,000 without accounting for $75,000 in site improvements. What is the probable sales price under the cost approach if the effective age of the building is 15 years, rounded to the nearest thousand?

   a. $3,549,000
   b. $3,474,000
   c. $3,315,000
   d. $3,240,000

6. A buyer is interested in purchasing a church that has 4,500 square feet, is 30 years old with a economic life of 85 years. The cost to build new is $200 per square foot. The broker, using the sales comparison approach determined the probable sales price of the land at $355,000. What is the probable sales price under the cost approach if the effective age of the building is 10 years, rounded to the nearest thousand?

   a. $ 582,000
   b. $ 794,000
   c. $ 937,000
   d. $1,149,000

VALUATION – INCOME APPROACH / INCOME CAPITALIZATION

This approach is often used by commercial brokers and licensed appraisers. The income approach (aka Income Capitalization Approach or Direct Capitalization Approach) is the primary method used to estimate the present value of properties that produce rental income.

Capitalization is the process of converting net operating income into an indication of value. Properties included in this category include apartment complexes, single-family rental homes, office buildings, shopping malls, parking garages, leased industrial plants, and individual properties occupied by commercial tenants. With this method you use anticipated future gross income. Effective gross income may also be called total anticipated revenue.

The value of the property is estimated by capitalizing Net Operating Income (NOI) into present value. The value of the property is directly related to the anticipated revenue and overall operating expenses.

For example, an apartment complex has a potential gross income of $1,350,000 if it were rented 100% of the time (no vacancy rate). If vacancy and collection losses amount to 6% of gross potential income. The gross effective income would be $1,350,000 x 0.94 or $1,269,000. If the building had $523,400 in operating expenses and the appraiser estimated the cap rate to be 12%, how much is the property worth?

Net Operating Income: $1,269,000 - $523,400 = $745,600
Value = Income ÷ Cap Rate: $745,600 ÷ .12 = $6,213,333.

The NOI or Net Operating Income is a way to determine the value of properties that produce income. This method involves the acronym above in the following order:

Gross Income	GI
Vacancy & Collections	- V&C
--------------	----------
Effective Gross Income	EGI
Less Operating Expenses	- Op Exp
--------------	--------------
Net Operating Income	NOI

Once the NOI is determined, the value of the property is determined by the following:

NOI / Capitalization Rate = Value

It is highly recommended that you study the T-bar below as it will help you answer math calculation and non-calculation problems.

Net Operating Income

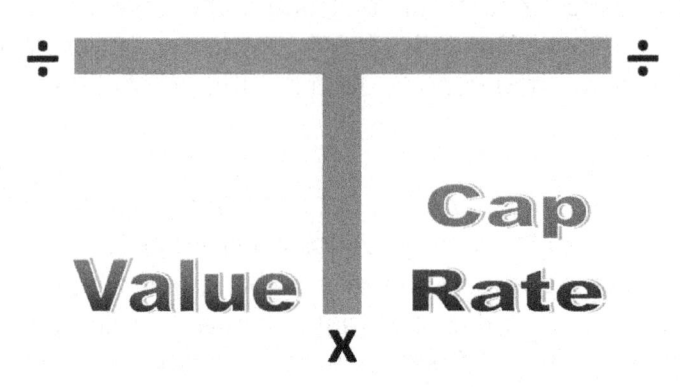

$$\text{Value} = \frac{\text{NOI}}{\text{Cap Rate}} \quad \text{Cap Rate} = \frac{\text{NOI}}{\text{Value}} \quad \text{NOI} = \text{Value} \times \text{Cap Rate}$$

Example 1. What is the value of a building with an NOI of $275,000 and a capitalization rate of 12%?

Value = NOI ÷ Cap Rate: $275,000 ÷ 12% = $2,291,667

Example 2. What is the cap rate if the NOI is $66,000 and the value of the building is $715,000?

Cap Rate = NOI ÷ Value: $66,000 ÷ $715,000 = 0.0923 or 9.23%

Example 3. An apartment complex has 25 units that rent for $900 per month, and 15 units that rent for $825 per month. Vacancy and collection losses are 4% of gross income. The management fee is 8% of effective gross income. The property has the following expenses: $77,000 in debt service, $23,000 in maintenance and repairs, $85,000 in other operating expenses and $60,000 in depreciation expenses. If the capitalization rate is 12%, what is the value of the building rounded to the nearest thousand?

First Calculate NOI:
GI – V&C = EGI – Operating Expense = NOI
GI: (25 X $900 X 12) + (15 X $825 X 12) = $270,000 + 148,500 = $418,500
V&C: GI $418,500 X 4% = $16,740
EGI: $401,760
 - MGT Fee: $32,141 ($401,760 X 8%)
 - Op Exp: $108,000 ($23,000 + $85,000)
NOI: $261,619

Value: NOI $261,619 ÷ Cap Rate 12% = $2,180,160, rounded $2,180,000

Problems for you to Solve (solutions page 100):

1. An appraiser is seeking to calculate the capitalization rate on a property. The correct formula is:

    a. Sales price divided by annual rent
    b. Net operating income divided by value
    c. Loan divided by value
    d. Before tax cash flow divided by equity

2. Stephen owns a property with an annual gross income of $400,000. The property experienced a 4% vacancy and collection loss, operating expenses of $275,000 and depreciation of $25,000. What is the value of the property, rounded to the nearest thousand if the capitalization rate is 8%?

    a. $ 1,050,000
    b. $ 1,363,000
    c. $10,500,000
    d. $13,625,000

3. Kelly wants to purchase a property with total anticipated revenue of $300,000 with a capitalization rate of 6%. The property experienced a 3% vacancy and collection loss, $175,000 operating expense and debt service of $40,000. What is the net operating income for the property, rounded to the nearest thousand?

    a. $ 116,000
    b. $ 125,000
    c. $1,933,000
    d. $2,083,000

4. A buyer is interested in a property that has an effective gross income of $890,000 with 5% vacancy and collection loss, depreciation expense $45,000, management fee 10% of effective gross income, debt service $70,000 and other operating expenses of $525,000. What is the value of the building if the capitalization rate is 14%, rounded to the nearest thousand?

    a. $1,971,000
    b. $1,654,000
    c. $1,650,000
    d. $1,471,000

5. John is purchasing a 15-unit apartment building where the rent is $1,500 per month per unit. The property has 6% vacancy and collection, management fee which is 12% of effective gross income, property taxes $24,000, debt service of $31,000, and other operating expenses of $99,000. What is the net operating income for this property?

   a. $100,344
   b. $116,544
   c. $124,344
   d. $130,800

6. Suzette is purchasing a 20-unit apartment building that rents for $1,450 per unit per month. On average 2 units will be vacant for the year and $2,900 of rent will not be collected. The management fee is 8% of effective gross income. The property has depreciation expense $25,000, utilities expense $55,000, debt service of $22,500, property taxes $60,000 and other operating expense of $85,000. What is the value of the property if the capitalization rate of 9%, rounded to the nearest thousand?

   a. $ 950,000
   b. $ 979,000
   c. $1,222,000
   d. $1,613,000

VALUATION – INCOME APPROACH – GROSS RENT (INCOME) MULTIPLIER

A gross rent multiplier is used to find the value of an investment property with 4 or less units based on monthly rent. The gross income multiplier is a similar calculation used for properties whose annual income comes from non-rental sources.

Gross rent (monthly) X gross rent multiplier = Value (Sales Price)
Gross Income (yearly) X gross income multiplier = Value (Sales Price)

Sales Price ÷ Monthly Rent = Gross Rent Multiplier
Sales Price ÷ Annual Rent = Gross Income Multiplier

Example 1. A property is valued at $560,000 with a gross yearly income of $60,000. What is the gross rent multiplier? If a similar property has gross yearly income of $70,000, what is the probable sales price of that building?

Monthly Rent: $60,000 ÷ 12 = $5,000
GRM: SP $560,000 ÷ $5,000 = 112

Similar Property Monthly Rent: $70,000 ÷ 12 = $5,833.33
Similar Property Probable Sales Price: $5,833.33 X 112 = $653,333.33

Example 2. An investor is looking to buy a property with annual gross income of $450,000. Similar comparable properties have a monthly gross rent multiplier of 122.5. What is the value of the building?

Monthly Income: $450,000 ÷ 12 = $37,500
Value: $37,500 X 122.5 = $4,593,750

Example 3. What is the gross income multiplier if the sales price of a building is $3,250,000 and the gross yearly income is $316,000.

GIM: SP $3,250,000 ÷ GI $316,000 = 10.28

Example 4. A property sold for $800,000 and has annual rent of $120,000. What is the gross rent multiplier?

Monthly Income: $120,000 ÷ 12 = $10,000
GRM: Sales Price $800,000 ÷ Monthly Rent $10,000 = 80

Problems for you to Solve (solutions page 102):

1. A property has gross income of $175,000 per year and sells for $2,100,000. What is the gross income multiplier?

    a. 12
    b. 120
    c. 144
    d. 1,440

2. An appraiser has determined that property in this area have an average gross rent multiplier of 250. The subject property rents for $750 per month. What is the estimate of market value for the property?

   a. $ 187,500
   b. $ 375,000
   c. $1,125,000
   d. $2,250,000

3. A 5-unit commercial property has an annual gross income of $250,000. The property recently sold for $2,000,000. What is the indicated gross rent multiplier?

   a. 8
   b. 40
   c. 96
   d. 480

4. An investor requires a 12.5% cap rate. They have identified a comparable property that recently sold for $3,750,000 with $360,000 of annual gross income. The property the investor is interested wants to purchase rents for $35,000 per month. What is the indicated value of the property given the information above?

   a. $ 364,583
   b. $2,880,000
   c. $3,360,000
   d. $4,375,000

5. What is gross rent multiplier for a duplex that rents for $2,700 per unit and sold for $810,000?

   a. 12.5
   b. 75.0
   c. 150
   d. 300

6. What is gross income multiplier for a triplex that rents for $2,100 per unit and sold for $743,400?

   a. 9.8333
   b. 29.500
   c. 118.00
   d. 354.00

FEDERAL INCOME TAXATION

This is for informational purposes only. There are no math problems to solve, however questions will be asked on how basis and amount realized are calculated.

The sale of property is treated as ordinary income and any gain will be taxed by the IRS. At closing the attorney will prepare a 1099-S of the seller's proceeds of the sale. This is filed with the Internal Revenue Service

BASIS is a key term that you must understand, which is another name for purchase price. This may be testing on the exam.

The COST BASIS of property is the owner's initial cost (purchase price plus allowable closing expenses). The owner can add to the cost basis for any physical improvements such as a new roof, room addition or other physical capital improvement to the property that adds value or extends the life of the property. This is called the <u>adjusted basis</u>.

Example 1. Able and his wife sell their home for $270,000. They can deduct closing costs that can be allocated to purchasing the property (but not to obtain the loan) include the closing attorney's fees and recording fee, which equal $1,475. A year later they have their home professionally pressure washed for $4,000. A year later they put on a $35,000 addition, install all new windows for $9,500 and update/remodel the kitchen for $12,000. Ten years later they replace the roof for $15,000.

Calculate the adjusted basis:

$270,000	**Purchase Price**
$ 1,475	**Allowable Closing Costs**
$ 35,000	**Addition to Home**
$ 9,500	**New Windows**
$ 12,000	**Updated Kitchen**
$ 15,000	**New Roof**
$197,025	**Adjusted Basis (remember this term)**

The $4,000 for pressure washing is not allowed because it is considered normal maintenance.

When the property is sold, the sales price less any closing expenses minus capital improvements can reduce the capital gain. If the person selling the property is single the exemption is $250,000, if married the exemption is $500,000.

There are some restrictions to this tax benefit. The seller must have occupied the property as a primary residence for 2 years of the previous five. And, the exemption is only available once every 2 years.

GAIN ON SALE - Percentage

You may be asked to calculate the percentage gain for a property. It is calculated as follows:

Sales Price – Original Purchase Price = Gain
Gain ÷ Original Purchase Price = % Gain

Or in a less nice way:
(New – Old) ÷ Old

Example 1. If I buy a property for $150,000 and sell it for $254,000 two years later, what was my percentage gain?

Gain: $254,000 - $150,000 = $104,000
Percentage Gain: $104,000 ÷ $150,000 = 0.6933 or 69.33%

Example 2. If I purchase a property for $250,000 and sell it 3 years later for $375,000, what was percentage loss?

Gain: $375,000 - $250,000 = $125,000
Percentage Gain: $125,000 ÷ $250,000 = .5 or 50%

Problems for you to Solve (solutions page 103):

1. A seller listed their property for $105,000 that ultimately sold for $100,000. If her cost was 80% of the listing price, what is the percent profit?
    a. 16%
    b. 19%
    c. 22%
    d. 25%

2. A couple listed their vacation home for $425,000, which ultimately sold for $412,500. If they originally purchased the property for $375,000, what is the percent profit?
    a. 9%
    b. 10%
    c. 13%
    d. 20%

GAIN IN EQUITY - Percentage

Gain in equity questions will require you to perform some initial calculations before you can calculate the percentage gain in equity from the date of purchase. First you will need to determine the current fair market value of the property given the purchase price and percentage increase from the date of purchase. Next determine the current mortgage balance based on the initial mortgage balance and a given reduction of the mortgage balance.

Recall that **equity** is calculated by taking the Fair Market Value of the property and subtracting the loan balance. When you purchase a property, the sales price is considered the fair market value and the down payment is considered the amount of equity.

Example 1. A buyer purchases a property for $200,000 by obtaining a conventional mortgage with an 80% LTV. Over the past 2 years the property has appreciated by 15% and the mortgage balance decreased by 10%. What is the percentage change in equity?

Initial Equity: A property with an 80% LTV required a 20% down payment. The down payment is the initial equity. $200,000 X 20% = $40,000
Initial Loan Amount: $200,000 - $40,000 = $160,000

FMV Increase: $200,000 X 15% = $30,000
New Fair Market Value: $200,000 + $30,000 = $230,000
Mortgage Balance Reduction: $160,000 X 10% = $16,000
Current Mortgage Balance: $160,000 - $16,000 = $144,000
New Equity: $230,000 - $144,000 = $86,000

Percentage Change: Recall (New – Old) / Old
($86,000 - $40,000) / $40,000 = 1.15 or 115%

Example 2. A property originally sold for $350,000 with the buyer making a 10% down payment. The property has appreciated by 30% over the past 5 years and the loan has decreased by 20%. What is the percentage increase in equity?

Initial Equity: $350,000 X 10% = $35,000
Initial Loan Amount: $350,000 X 90% = $315,000

FMV Increase: $350,000 X 30% = $105,000
New Fair Market Value: $350,000 + $105,000 = $455,000
Mortgage Balance Reduction: $315,000 X 20% = $63,000
Current Mortgage Balance: $315,000 - $63,000 = $252,000
New Equity: $455,000 - $252,000 = $203,000
Percentage Change: ($203,000 - $35,000) / $35,000 = 4.8 or 480%

Problems for you to Solve (solutions page 103):

1. A property was purchased for $650,000 by making at $50,000 down payment. The property appreciated by 40% and the mortgage balance decreased by 25% over the past 7 years. What is the percentage change in equity?

    a. 8.2%
    b. 16.4%
    c. 410%
    d. 820%

2. A property sold for $425,000 with the buyer obtaining an 85% LTV mortgage at 5.5% interest for 30 years. The property appreciated by 18% and the mortgage decreased by 12% over the past 5 years. What is the percentage change in equity?

    a. 1.89%
    b. 3.76%
    c. 189%
    d. 376%

CALCULATING THE PROPERTY MANAGER'S FEE

The property management fee is typically paid based upon the amount of rent collected. In certain circumstances a flat fee may be charged, however it is unlikely that this will be tested in this manner on the license exam.

Example 1. A duplex rents for $2,400 per unit. The property management fee is 10% of gross rent collected. The property experienced a 6% vacancy & collection loss. How much did the property manager earn for the year?

$2,400 x 2 units x 12 months = $57,600 Annual Gross Income
$57,600 x 0.06 = $3,456 Vacancy and Collection
$57,600 - $3,456 = $54,144 Effective Gross Income
Property Management fee is 10% of Effective Gross Income
$54,144 x 0.10 = **$5,414.40 property management fee for the year.**

Example 2. A 14-unit apartment building rents for $1,900 per unit. There is a 5% vacancy and collection loss. What is the property manager's fee for the year if they charge 12% of effective gross income?

$1,900 / unit x 14 units x 12 months = $319,200 Annual Gross Income

$319,200 X 5% = $15,960 Vacancy and Collection
$319,200 - $15,960 = $303,240 Effective Gross Income
$303,240 x 0.12 (property management fee) = $36,388.80 Annual PM Fee

Problems for you to Solve (solutions page 104):

1. John is hired to manage a property that rents for $1,200 per month. The property not experienced a vacancy and collection loss, however other rental properties in the area typically lose 5%. What is the monthly management fee if John earns 12% of rent collected?

    a. $ 137
    b. $ 144
    c. $1,642
    d. $1,728

2. A property has effective gross income of $250,000 with a 4% vacancy and collection loss. The owner and firm have agreed to a management fee of 9% of gross rent collected. How much will the firm earn for the year?

    a. $ 9,100
    b. $10,000
    c. $20,475
    d. $22,500

3. Amy is managing a 50-unit apartment complex where each unit rents for $1,000 per month. The anticipated vacancy and collection loss is 6% and the property manager is paid 12% of collected rent. What is the projected annual income for the property manager?

    a. $72,000
    b. $67,680
    c. $ 6,000
    d. $ 5,640

4. A 25-unit apartment complex has 15 units that rent for $1,200 per month and 10 units that rent for $1,500. Vacancy and collection losses are 3% of gross rental income. The property has $4,000 per month of operating expenses and $2,500 per monthly debt service payments. How much will the property manager be paid annual if the fee charged is 10% of effective gross income?

    a. $20,952
    b. $21,600
    c. $38,412
    d. $39,600

5. A broker is managing a duplex that rents for $1,800 per unit. The units on average are vacant for one month of the year. Assuming that rent was paid in full for the month of June, what is the amount of compensation paid to the broker when the owner has agreed to pay 12% of gross rent received or $75, whichever is greater?

    a. $ 216
    b. $ 432
    c. $2,376
    d. $4,752

6. Kevin owns a 100-unit apartment building, whose units rent for $1,250 per month. On average 8 units are vacant throughout the year and collection loses are $3,750. What is the annual compensation for the property manager when the management fee is 8% of the gross rent received?

    a. $110,100
    b. $110,400
    c. $119,700
    d. $120,000

PERCENTAGE LEASE (RETAIL BUSINESS)

In retail leases the tenant pays a base rent plus a percentage of gross sales typically over a stated amount. The tenant reports gross sales to the landlord each month or quarterly depend on the lease agreement.

The advantage of doing this allows the tenant to have a lower base rent when initially starting the business, while paying an agreed upon percentage of all sales over a certain amount allows the owner to participate in the business's success. This also helps the Landlord make the property more attractive to other retail tenants. This is how calculate office/retail space rent:

The fixed base annual rent plus a percentage of gross sales over a given amount will equal the monthly and/or annual adjusted rent.

Example 1. Find the annual rent if the base rent is $1,000 per month, plus 5% of annual sales which exceed $450,000, when the annual sales volume is $750,000.

$1,000 x 12 months = $12,000 (base annual rent)
750,000 – 450,000 = 300,000 x .05 = $15,000 (annual percentage)
Base rent ($12,000) + Adjusted percentage ($15,000) = $30,000 annual rent

Example 2. A retail store agreed to pay a percentage lease of $1,700 monthly and 7% of gross sales over $75,000. If gross sales for the year are $150,000, what would the total lease amount paid for the year be?

Base Rent: $1,700 X 12 = $20,400
Percentage: ($150,000 - $75,000) X 7% = $5,250
Total Rent: $20,400 + $5,250 = $25,650

Example 3. Glenn owns a commercial building with two leased units, both on percentage leases. The first space pays a fixed rent amount of $2,500 per month, and 4% of gross sales over $175,000. The second space pays fixed rent of $1,800 per month, and 6.5% of gross sales over $85,000. If the first space gross sales are $250,000 and the second space gross sales are $205,000, how much will Glenn make in total annual rent for both units?

Unit 1: Base Rent: $2,500 X 12 = $30,000
Unit 1: Percentage: ($250,000 - $175,000) X 4% = $3,000
Unit 1: Total Rent: $30,000 + $3,000 = $33,000

Unit 2: Base Rent: $1,800 X 12 = $21,600
Unit 2: Percentage: ($205,000 - $85,000) X 6.5% = $7,800
Unit 2: Total Rent: $21,600 + $7,800 = $29,400

Total Rent: $33,000 + $29,400 = $62,400

Problems for you to Solve (solutions page 105):

1. A lease calls for a monthly minimum (Base) rent of $1,200 plus 4% of annual gross sales over $500,000. What is the annual rent if annual gross sales are projected to be $900,000?

    a. $34,400
    b. $39,400
    c. $30,400
    d. $14,400

2. A lease calls for a monthly base rent of $15 per square foot. The space to be rented is 1,400 sf. The landlord is charging 5.5% of annual gross sales above $350,000, and annual gross sales are anticipated to be $500,000. What is the projected annual rent?

    a. $ 8,250
    b. $21,000
    c. $29,250
    d. $21,688

3. Starbucks is looking to rent a space that is $12 per square foot in a space that is 2500 square feet. The owner of the building will charge 4% of any gross sales above $450,000. Starbucks expects annual gross sales to reach $950,000. What is the annual estimated rent?

    a. $29,000
    b. $38,000
    c. $41,000
    d. $50,000

End – Solutions next page

SOLUTIONS
PROPERTY TAXATION

1. B - $2,787. Property taxes in North Carolina are charged per $100 of assessed value.

   Assessed Value ÷ 100 X Tax Rate = Tax for Year
   $185,800 ÷ 100 X $1.50 = $2,787

2. C - $4,639.35. Property taxes are charge on the assessed value, not the sales price or fair market value. When a property is located in the city, the owner will pay both city and county taxes. It is important to read the question carefully to determine if the property is located in the city or only in the county.

   Assessed Value ÷ 100 X Tax Rate = Tax for Year
   Tax Rate: $1.35 + $0.62 = $1.97
   $235,500 ÷ 100 X $1.97 = $4,639.35

3. C - $121. It is important to read the problem to ensure you are solving for the correct answer. Taxation questions can seek the yearly or monthly taxes for a property. In this question it is monthly. Note that the year tax amount was given as one of the answer choices.

   Assessed Value ÷ 100 X Tax Rate = Tax for Year
   $100,000 ÷ 100 = 1,000 X $1.45 = $1,450
   Monthly Tax: $1,450 ÷ 12 = $121

4. D - $3,460. A property that is located in the city with pay both city and county taxes. Property taxes are paid on the total assessed value of the home and the land.

   Assessed Value ÷ 100 X Tax Rate = Tax for Year
   $185,000 ÷ 100 X $1.87 = $3,459.50

5. C - $2,340. A property located in the city will pay both city and county taxes. Property taxes are paid on the assessed value, not the market value of the property.

   Assessed Value ÷ 100 X Tax Rate = Tax for Year
   Assessed Value: $240,000 X 75% = $180,000

Tax for year: $180,000 ÷ 100 X $1.30 = $2,340

6. B - $3,063. Property taxes are based on the assessed value, not the market value of the property.

   Assessed Value ÷ 1000 X Mills Rate = Tax for Year
   Assessed Value: $175,000 X 70% = $122,500
   Tax for Year = $122,500 ÷ 1,000 X 25 Mills = $3,062.50

AREA PROBLEMS

1. A – 0.86 acres. The area of a lot is calculated by multiplying the length X the width. Recall that an acre has 43,560 square feet.

   Area: 150' X 250' = 37,500 sq.ft.
   Acreage: 37,500 ÷ 43,560 = 0.8608 acres

2. D - $48,750. The first call dimension is the front footage for a property, while the second call describes the lots depth.

   Lot Price: 250 X $195 = $48,750

3. B – 261.36'. The area of a lot is calculated by taking the length X the width. This problem is asking for the depth/width of the property.

   Area = Length X Width…so to solve for the width take the Area ÷ Length
   Area: 43,560 X .9 = 39,204 sqft.
   39,204 ÷ 150 = 261.36'

4. B - $16,529. In order to calculate commission we must calculate the sales price of the property, so we first need to determine the acreage.

   Square Footage: 200' X 300' = 60,000 sqft.
   Acreage: 60,000 ÷ 43,560 = 1.3774 acres
   Sales Price: 1.3774 X $150,000 = $206,612
   Commission: $206,612 X 8% = $16,529

5. A - $1,292,000. In order to calculate the cost of the 2 lots, we must determine the total square footage. Then we must calculate the acreage.

   Lot 1 area: 5,280' X 5,280' = 27,878,400 sqft.
   Lot 2 area: 511.23' X 511.23' = 261,356 sqft.
   Total Area: 27,878,400 sqft. + 261,356 sqft. = 28,139,756 sqft.
   Acreage: 28,139,756 ÷ 43,560 = 646 acres
   Cost: 646 acres X $2,000 per acre = $1,292,000

6. A – 2.99 acres. It is helpful to draw a picture of the two lots. Then find out how many square feet are in Lot A, then divide by depth to determine the front footage. Since both lots have the same footage and the problem gave us the depth of lot 2, we can calculate the square footage of the lot and then divide by 43,560 to determine the acreage.

   Lot A Front Footage: 3.45 acres X 43,560 sqft. = 150,282 sqft ÷ 900' = 166.98'
   Lot B Square Footage: 166.98' X 780' = 130,244.4 sqft.
   Lot B Acreage: 130,244.4 ÷ 43,560 = 2.99 acres

7. D - $840. The front footage is the first number given for the lot dimensions. In this instance 165'. In order to calculate the cost per front foot, take the sales price and divide by front footage.

   $138,600 ÷ 165' = $840

8. C – 7.10 Acres. Since the parcel is split into 2 equal parts, calculate the square footage and divide by 2, as the problem asks for the acreage of EACH lot. Then divide that amount by 43,560 to calculate the acreage.

   Square footage 1 Tract: 750' X 825' ÷ 2 = 309,375 sqft.
   Acreage 1 Tract: 309,375 ÷ 43,560 = 7.10 acres

9. D – 16,627. If an acre contains 43,560 square feet, than 0.3817 acres can be calculated by multiplying the two numbers.

   43,560 X 0.3817 = 16,627 sqft.

RECTANGULAR SURVEY METHOD

1. B – 20 acres. Recall that there are 640 acres in a section. When a problem says "and" or there is a "semi-colon", then it means that you add the 2 lots together. Since the lot denominators are the same we can calculate the acreage of one lot and multiply it by 2 for the answer.

   Acreage Section 14: 640 ÷ 4 ÷ 4 ÷ 4 = 10 acres
   Acreage Both Lots: 10 X 2 = 20 acres

2. C - $1,050,000. Recall there are 640 acres in a section. When a problem says "and" or there is a "semi-colon", then add the 2 figures together to obtain the total square footage of the lot.

   Section 17 acreage: 640 ÷ 4 ÷ 4 ÷ 2 = 20 acres
   Total Acreage: 20 + 10 = 30 acres
   Cost: 30 X $35,000 = $1,050,000

3. C – 40 acres. Recall that there are 640 acres in a section. First multiply the denominators. Then take 640 acres and divide by the denominators to determine the acreage.

   Acreage: 640 ÷ 4 ÷ 2 ÷ 2 = 40 acres

SQUARE YARDS

1. C – 66.44 SY. First you need to calculate the total square footage of carpet needed. Then recall that a square yard = 9 square feet (3' X 3').

   Sq.Ft. Living Room: 22' X 17' = 374 sq.ft.
   Sq.Ft. Family Room: 16' X 14' = 224 sq.ft.
   Total Sq.Ft.: 374 + 224 = 598 sq.ft.
   Square Yards: 598 ÷ 9 = 66.44 SY

2. D - $1,202. To calculate square yards recall that there are 9 square feet to a square yard.

Family Room Sq.Ft.: 22' X 15' = 330
Family Room SY: 330 ÷ 9 = 36.6667
Family Room Cost: 36.6667 X $18 = $660

Den Sq.Ft: 15' X 13' = 195
Den SY: 195 ÷ 9 = 21.6667
Den Cost: 21.6667 X $25 = $541.66

Total Cost: $660 + $541.66 = $1201.66, rounded $1,202

3. A - $12,185. It is important to use the appropriate measurement when calculating the cost of the concrete (per square yard) and flashing (per square foot). To calculate square yards, recall there are 9 square feet in a square yard (3' X 3').

   Patio Sq.Ft.: 25' X 15' = 375
   Flashing Cost: 375 X $25 = $9,375

   Patio SY: 375 ÷ 9 = 41.6667
   Concrete Cost: 41.6667 X $45 = $1,875

   Project Cost: $9,375 flashing + $1,875 concrete + $935 labor = $12,185

4. B - $1,363. To calculate square yards recall that there are 9 square feet in a square yard (3' X 3').

   Square Yards: 250 ÷ 9 = 28.7777
   Cost of Linoleum: 28.7777 X $47.35 = $1,363

EXCISE TAX

1. B - $207. To calculate the excise tax on the sale of the property, take the sales price and divide by $500, then round up.

   $103,250 ÷ 500 = $206.50, rounded to $207

2. C - $730. Excise tax is based on the sales price and in North Carolina is $1 per $500 of sales price.

   $365,000 ÷ $500 = $730

3. B - $555. You must first calculate the sales price of the property before calculating excise tax. If the home sold for 6% less than the list price, the sales price is 94% of list price (100% - 6%).

   Sales Price: $295,000 X 94% = $277,300
   Excise: $277,300 ÷ $500 = $554.60, rounded to $555

COMMISSION

1. D - $4243. Commission is often based upon the sales price of the home. This problem is straightforward as there typically is a split between the listing brokerage and selling brokerage and then a split between the brokerage and the firm.

   Total Commission: $110,000 X 6% = $6,600
   Franchise Fee: $6,600 X 6% = $396
   Commission Split: $6,600 - $396 = $6,204 X 70% = $4,242.80

2. C - $12,760. Depending on a broker's independent contractor agreement, the broker may be required to split all compensation with the firm. In this instance the sales commission must be split, however the bonus is paid to the buyer's agent at 100%. The problem states that the compensation will be split. When no instructions have been given about how it will be split, the split is 50/50.

   Total Commission: Sales Price $480,000 X 3.5% Commission Rate = $16,800
   Commission Split: $16,800 X 70% = $11,760
   Total Buyer's Agent Compensation: $11,760 + $1,000 = $12,760

3. C - $3,780. Commission is typically paid on the sales price of the property.

   Total Commission: $90,000 X 7% = $6,300
   Commission Split: $6,300 X 60% = $3,780

4. B - $76,800. This problem is similar to calculating the sales price needed to cover commission. Take the sellers net after paying commission and divide it by the difference between 100% less the commission percentage.

   Sales Price 100% - Commission 7% = 93%
   Sales Price Less Commission $71,424 ÷ 93% = $76,800

5. A - $6,623. The commission is tiered and therefore you need to perform multiple calculations and then add up the results.

   Tier 1: $100,000 X 6.5% = $6,500
   Tier 2: $100,000 X 5.0% = $5,000
   Tier 3: $165,000 X 4.5% = $7,425

   Total Commission: $18,925
   Commission to Selling Firm: $18,925 ÷ 2 = $9,462.50
   Commission to Buyer's Agent: $9,462.50 X 70% = $6,623

6. C - $234,000. The commission is tiered, therefore you need to perform multiple calculations and then add up the result.

   Tier 1: $1,000,000 X 7% = $ 70,000
   Tier 2: $1,000,000 X 6% = $ 60,000
   Tier 3: $2,600,000 X 4% = $104,000 ($4,600,000 - $2,000,000)

   Total Commission: $234,000

SALES PRICE NEED FOR SELLER TO NET $X

1. C - $146,300. When calculating the sellers net, add up the known seller fees. The one part missing is the amount of commission. It is a common mistake to multiply this low number by the rate of commission and add the two numbers together – however the known fees are all expenses less commission, not the sales price.

   Seller Known Expenses and Net: $85,000 + $2,500 + $50,000 = $137,500
   Percentage of Sales Price less Commission: SP 100% - Comm 6% = 94%
   Sales Price: $137,500 ÷ 94% = $146,276.60, rounded to $146,300

2. C - $320,400. Add up the seller know expenses. The seller typically pays CD&E – Commission, deed prep and excise tax.

   Seller Known Expenses and Net: $45,000 + $3,000 + $250,000 = $298,000
   Percentage of Sale Price less Commission: SP 100% - Comm 7% = 93%
   Sales Price: $298,000 ÷ .93 = $320,430.10, rounded $320,400

3. D - $326,300. Add up known seller expenses and desired net. The assumption fee is a buyer's expense so this is ignored.

   Seller Known Expenses and Net: $75,000 + $223,500 + $5,000 = $303,500
   Percentage of Sales Price less Commission: SP 100% - Comm 7% = 93%
   Sales Price: $303,500 ÷ 93% = $326,344.08, rounded to $326,300

4. C - $240,100. Add up known seller expenses and desired net. Loan origination is a buyer's expense and therefore should be ignored.

   Seller Known Expenses and Net:
   $45,000 + $175,900 + $150 + $50 + $7,000 = $228,100
   Percentage of Sales Price less Commission: SP 100% - Comm 5% = 95%
   Sales Price: $228,100 ÷ 95% = $240,105.25, rounded to $240,100

LIVING AREA SQUARE FOOTAGE

1. B - $141.30. To calculate the cost per square foot divide the purchase price of the home by the square footage. The mortgage amount is a distractor and is not applicable to the problem.

   Cost per Square Foot: $325,000 ÷ 2,300 = $141.30

2. A – 1,640. In order for square footage to be included in living area, it must be heated, finished and directly accessible. A deck does not meet this requirement. A great room is heated, finished and directly accessible based on the illustration and therefore would be included. Some distances in the problem have not been provided, however you can determine the length based upon other measurements given.

   Length of Large Rectangle: 65' – 15' = 50' (note: 15' length of deck)
   Length of Great Room: 50' – 12' – 12' = 26'
   Large Rectangle Square Footage: 50' X 25' = 1,250
   Great Room Square Footage: 26' X 15' = 390
   Living Area Square Footage: 1,250 + 390 = 1,640

3. C – 2,062. When calculating square footage always check the problem for unfinished square footage to back out such as a garage, deck or porch. This problem does differentiate the space and therefore is all heated, finished and directly accessible. You do not typically round up square footage or lot size.

Base of Triangle: 65' – 50' = 15'
Large Rectangle Square Footage: 65' X 30' = 1,950
Triangle Square Footage: 1/2 X 15' X 15' = 212.5
Living Area Square Footage: 1,950 + 112 = 2,062

POINTS and YIELD TO LENDER

1. C - $5,600. Points are paid on the loan amount, not the sales price. They represent prepaid interest paid to lower the stated rate on the mortgage note. One point equates to 1% of the loan amount.

    Points: 2 points = 2% of the loan amount
    Points Paid: Loan $280,000 X 2% = $5,600

2. A - $3,187.50. Points are paid on the loan amount, not the sales price.

    Points: 1.5 points = 1.5% of the loan amount
    Points Paid: Loan $250,000 X 1.5% = $3,187.50

3. D – 6.25%. When a buyer pays discount points it lowers the stated rate on the mortgage note. The buyer is prepaying interest which increases the yield to the lender. One discount point costs a borrower 1% of the loan amount and in return the borrower will get a 1/8 or .125 change in the interest rate.

    Change in rate: 2/8 = .25
    Yield to Lender: Stated rate 6 + .25 = 6.25%

FACTORS and PITI PAYMENTS

1. In order to calculate the PI payment you must take the loan amount divide it by 1,000 and multiply by the factor (amortization rate).

    Monthly PI Payment: $240,000 ÷ 1,000 X 6.99 = $1,677.60

2. The PITI payment consists of principal, interest, taxes and insurance. Using the monthly PI payment above, the only missing piece is monthly taxes and insurance.

   Monthly TI: $4,500 ÷ 12 = $375
   Monthly PITI: $1,677.60 + $375 = $2,052.60

3. The PI payment is based upon the loan amount, not the sales price.

   Loan Amount: $325,000 X 95% LTV = $308,750
   Monthly PI Payment: $308,750 1,000 X 7.34 = $2,266.23

4. Using the PI Payment from problem 3 all that is needed is the calculation of monthly taxes and insurance.

   Monthly TI: ($5,600 + $1,200) ÷ 12 = $566.67
   Monthly PITI: $2,266.23 + $566.67 = $2,832.90

TOTAL INTEREST PAID – Over Life of Loan

1. B - $145,068. When calculating the total interest over the life of the loan, you must know the loan payment. Sometimes the payment is provided and sometimes you will need to calculate it. The factor or amortization rate is typically provided in the problem.

   Monthly PI Payment: $165,000 ÷ 1,000 X 5.22 = $861.30
   Total PI Payments: $861.30 X 360 = $310,068
   Total Interest Paid: $310,068 - $165,000 = $145,068

2. A - $87,626. In order to calculate total interest over the life of the loan, you must first calculate the loan amount. If the buyer makes a 3.5% down payment, then the LTV is 96.5%. The interest rate is a distractor and will not be used to solve the problem. Use the factor to calculate the monthly principal and interest. Subtract the original loan amount from the total PI payments to calculate total interest paid over the life of the loan.

   Loan Amount: $114,000 X 96.5% = $110,010
   Monthly PI Payment: $110,010 ÷ 1,000 X 4.9904 = $548.99
   Total PI Payments: $548.99 X 360 = $197,636
   Total Interest Paid: $197,636 - $110,010 = $87,626

3. D - $85,679. The term amortization rate is referring to the factor so either term could be used in a problem. In this problem both loans are for the same amount so there is no need to back out the original loan amount from both calculation in order to determine the difference in interest paid.

   15 Year Monthly PI Payment: $195,000 ÷ 1,000 X 6.135 = $1,196.33
   15 Year Total PI Payments: $1,196.33 X 180 = $215,339
   30 Year Monthly PI Payment: $195,000 ÷ 1,000 X 4.288 = $836.16
   30 Year Total PI Payments: $836.16 X 360 = $301,018

   Interest Savings: $301,018 - $215,339 = $85,679

4. A - $170,235. The only way to solve the problem is to calculate the monthly PI payment for both loans and multiply it by the respective loan terms. A common mistake is to calculate interest for the year and then multiply it by the number of years the money is borrowed. This method is wrong because the interest amount changes each year, going down as principal payments are applied (the loan amortizes).

   Loan Amount: $375,000 - $50,000 = $325,000

   15 Year Monthly PI Payment: $325,000 ÷ 1,000 X 7.53 = $2,447.25
   15 Year Total PI Payments: $2,447.25 X 180 = $440,504
   30 Year Monthly PI Payment: $325,000 ÷ 1,000 X 5.22 = $1,696.50
   30 Year Total PI Payments: $1,696.50 X 360 = $610,740

   Interest Savings: $610,740 - $440,504 = $170,235

BALANCE AFTER 1 PAYMENT

1. C - $174,779. The monthly PI payment is based upon the loan amount. The factor is a dollar amount per month per thousand dollars borrowed.

   Monthly PI Payment: 175 X 5.22 = $913.50
   Monthly Interest: $175,000 X 4.75% ÷ 12 = $692.71
   Principal Payment: $913.50 - $692.71 = $220.79
   New Balance: $175,000 - $220.79 = $174,779.21

2. B - $181,176. Unless already provided in the problem, the first step is to determine the loan amount and monthly PI payment. Next calculate the monthly interest by taking the loan times the rate divided by 12. Subtract the 2 to determine the amount of the payment to be applied to principal and subtract it from the loan amount.

   Loan Amount: $188,000 X 96.5% (or .965) = $181,420
   PI Payment: $181,420 ÷ 1,000 X 4.9904 = $905.36
   Monthly Interest: $181,420 X 4.375% (or .04375) ÷ 12 = $661.43
   Principal Payment: $905.36 - $661.43 = $243.93
   New Balance: $181,420 - $243.93 = $181,176.07

3. C - $224,613. It is important to calculate the loan amount even though the monthly payment has been provided. You only use the PI portion when amortizing a loan as the TI portion is deposited in an escrow account and paid out when taxes and insurance are due.

   Loan Amount: $249,900 X 90% (or .90) = $224,910
   PI Payment: $1,340 PITI - $200 TI = $1,140 ($2,400 ÷ 12 = $200 Monthly TI)
   Monthly Interest: $224,910 X 4.5% (or .045) ÷ 12 = $843.41
   Principal Payment: $1,140 - $843.41 = $296.59
   New Balance: $224,910 - $296.59 = $224,613.41

4. B - $707,107. It is important to calculate the loan amount to accurately calculate the PI payment and amortization. Taxes and Insurance are distractors and not need to solve the problem.

   Loan Amount: $885,000 X 80% (or .80) = $708,000
   PI Payment: $708,000 ÷ 1,000 X 5.22 = $3,695.76
   Monthly Interest: $708,000 X 4.75% (or .0475) ÷ 12 = $2,802.76
   Principal Payment: $3,695.76 - $2,802.76 = $893.26
   New Balance: $708,000 - $893.26 = $707,106.74

MORTGAGE QUALIFYING

1. A – I Only. When performing mortgage qualifying problems, expenses need to be split between Housing (PITI +HOA dues) and Total Debt (Housing + Long Term Debt). When determining if a borrower qualifies for a mortgage, they must qualify under both ratios. Caution: When answering I/II type questions you are evaluating each answer choice as correct vs. if the borrower qualifies overall.

Monthly Income: $66,000 ÷ 12 = $5,500
Maximum Housing: $5,500 X 28% = $1,540
Maximum Total Debt: $5,500 X 36% = $1,980

Actual Housing: $1,200 + $250 = $1,450 (qualify)
Actual Total Debt: $1,450 + $300 + $350 = $2,100 (does not qualify)

2. B - $2,333. The maximum PITI payment is the lower amount – in this instance the amount indicated under Housing. Long term debts limit the amount of money that a bank will lend to a borrower. It is important to calculate both housing and total debt. To determine the maximum PITI under total debt, subtract long term debts. Since you are calculating the maximum PITI payment you do not need use property taxes and insurance information provided.

Monthly Income: $100,000 ÷ 12 = $8,333
Maximum Housing: $8,333 X 28% = $2,333
Maximum Total Debt: $8,333 X 36% = $3,000
Maximum PITI Total Debt: $3,000 - $520 = $2,480

3. C – Both I and II. Housing expenses include PITI + HOA dues, as the homeowner association can foreclose on the property if the owner does not pay the dues.

Monthly Income: ($60,000 ÷ 12) + $4,500 = $9,500
Maximum Housing: $9,500 X 28% = $2,660
Maximum Total Debt: $9,500 X 36% = $3,420

Actual Housing: $1,600 + $400 + $200 + $50 = $2,250 (qualify)
Actual Total Debt: $2,250 + $800 + $300 + $50 = $3,400 (qualify)

4. B - $2,620. The maximum PITI payment is going to the lower of the 2. The factor and monthly T&I are distractors and are not need to answer the problem. The question is asking for the maximum PITI and therefore would include both the taxes and insurance.

Monthly Income: $120,000 ÷ 12 = $10,000
Max Housing: $10,000 X 28% = $2,800
Max Total Debt: $10,000 X 36% = $3,600
Max PITI Total Debt: $3,600 - $980 = $2,620

5. B - $7,426. When calculating minimum income needed to qualify it is the higher of the 2 amounts. Always double check to see if you are calculating monthly or yearly income.

   Loan Amount: $235,000 - $25,000 = $210,000
   PI Payment: $210,000 ÷ 1,000 X 7.46 = $1,566.60
   Housing: $1,566.60 + $416.67 = $1,983.27 (TI and Housing calculated by adding $3,500, $900 and $600 then ÷ by 12)
   Total Debt: $1,983.67 + $690 = $2,673.27 (Other Debt calculated by adding $330, $200 and $160)

   Minimum Income Housing: $1,983.27 ÷ 28% = $7,083
   Minimum Income Total Debt: $2,673.27 ÷ 36% = $7,426

6. B - $950. To calculate maximum additional long term debt, you must calculate maximum allowed total debt, subtract the housing payment, and then subtract any long-term debt given in the problem.

   Monthly Income: $175,000 ÷ 12 = $14,583
   Max Total Debt: $14,583 X 36% = $5,250
   Max Other Debt: $5,250 - $3,000 PI - $1,000 TI - $300 Car = $950

INTERIM / PREPAID INTEREST

1. C - $176. Interim / Prepaid interest is paid by the buyer to the bank from the day of closing through the end of the month. The lender will bill the remaining payments on a monthly basis. Interim/Prepaid interest is calculated for only one month. To determine the number of days the buyer will pay: 30 – day of closing + 1. Remember to add one because the bank is greedy.

   Daily Rate: Loan $192,000 X Rate 5.5% ÷ 360 = $29.3333
   Days: 30 – 25 + 1 = 6 days
   Interim / Prepaid Interest: $29.3333 X 6 = $176

2. C - $826.88. Interim / prepaid interest is charged from the day of closing through the end of the month. Interest is calculated based upon the loan amount, not the purchase price.

   Loan Amount: $315,000 X 90% = $283,500

Daily Rate: $238,500 X 5% ÷ 360 = $39.375
Days: 30 − 10 + 1 = 21 days
Interim / Prepaid Interest: $39.375 X 21 = $826.88

PRORATION - PROPERTY TAX PRORATION

1. A - Since the closing is after 9/1 and taxes are unpaid, use the double debit method where the attorney will pay the bill when the deed is recorded.

   Buyer Number of Days: (O) 24 + (ND) 60 = 84 days Buyer
   Daily Rate: $2,900 ÷ 360 = $8.0555
   Buyer Tax: $8.0555 X 84 = $676.67
   Seller Tax: $2,900 - $515.56 = $2,223.33
   Entry: Debit Buyer $676.67 / Debit Seller $2,223.33

2. D - Since the closing is before 9/1, taxes are unpaid, so the seller will be debited and buyer credit. The buyer will pay the tax bill when it becomes due.

   Seller Number of Days: (JF) 60 + (M) 14 = 74 Days
   Daily Rate: $4,500 ÷ 360 = $12.50
   Seller Tax: $12.50 X 74 = $925
   Entry: Debit Seller $925 / Credit Buyer $925

3. C - Since the closing is after 9/1 and the taxes have been paid, the buyer will reimburse the seller – so debit buyer / credit seller for the same amount.

   Buyer Number of Days: (N) 13 + (D) 30 = 43 Days
   Daily Rate: $3,300 ÷ 360 = $9.1667
   Buyer Tax: $9.1667 X 43 = $394.17
   Entry: Debit Buyer $394.17 / Credit Seller $394.17

4. A – Since the closing is after 9/1 and axes are unpaid the attorney will charge the buyer and seller their respective portion and pay the bill upon closing – double debit / different amounts. This question also requires the calculation of the property taxes for the year. Recall in NC property taxes are charged per $100 of assessed value and the assessed value only changes in revaluation years, not the property's sales price.

   Tax YR: AV $240,000 / 100 X TR $1.50 = $3,600

Buyer Days: (Sep) 9 + (OND) 90 = 99 Days
Daily Rate: $3,600 / 360 = $10.00
Tax Buyer: $10.00 X 99 Days = $990
Tax Seller: $3,600 - $990 = $2,610
Entry: Debit Buyer $990 / Debit Seller $2,610

5. B – Since the closing is before September 1 and taxes are unpaid the attorney will charge (debit) the seller and credit the buyer the same dollar amount. The seller pays the buyer for his/her number of days and the buyer will pay the full bill when it becomes due. Property taxes are based upon the assessed value. When a property is located in the county, the owner pays only county taxes. When a property is located in the city, the owner pays both city and county taxes. Since the property in this question is located in the county, we will ignore the city tax rate.

Tax YR: AV $960,000 / 100 X TR $0.75 = $7,200
Seller Days: (Jan) 30 + (Feb) 9 = 39 Days
Daily Rate: $7,200 / 360 = $20
Tax Seller: $20.00 X 39 = $780
Entry: Debit Seller $780 / Credit Buyer $780

6. C – Since closing is after September 1st and taxes have been paid by the seller, the buyer will need to reimburse the seller for the number of days that the buyer owns the property. Property taxes are based on the assessed value rather than the sales price.

AV: $480,000 X 90% = $432,000
Tax for Year: AV $432,000 / 100 X TR $1.25 = $5,400
Buyer Days: (Dec) 9
Daily Rate: $5,400 / 360 = $15
Buyer Tax: $15 X 9 = $135
Entry: Debit Buyer $135 / Credit Seller $135

RENT PRORATION

1. D - $833.33. Read the problem carefully. A duplex has 2 units and therefore rent must be multiplied by 2. The seller is paid through the day of closing unless the problem states otherwise. Since rent has been paid the seller needs to reimburse the buyer for the number of days the buyer will own the property.

Monthly Rent: $2,500 X 2 = $5,000
Daily Rent: $5,000 ÷ 30 = $166.6667
Buyer Days: 30 – 25 = 5 days
Buyer Entry: $166.6667 X 5 = $833.33 Debit Seller / Credit Buyer

2. C - $360. Make sure to read the problem carefully. A triplex has 3 units so make sure to multiply monthly rent by 3. The buyer will need to pay the seller and then can retain the full amount when the tenants pay the rental bill.

   Monthly Rent: $1,200 X 3 = $3,600
   Daily Rent: $3,600 ÷ 30 = $120
   Seller Days: 3
   Entry: $120 X 3 = $360 Debit Buyer / Credit Seller

3. B - $1,393.33. Make sure to read the problem carefully. A duplex has 3 units. Since the rent has been paid, the seller needs to reimburse the buyer for the number days the buyer will own the property.

   Monthly Rent: $1,100 X 2 = $2,200
   Daily Rent: $2,200 ÷ 30 = $73.3333
   Buyer Days: 30 – 11 = 19
   Entry: $73.3333 X 19 = $1,393.33 Debit Seller / Credit Buyer

HOA PRORATION

1. B – Debit Buyer $133.33 / Credit Seller $133.33. Unless stated otherwise, the seller pays through the day of closing. Since the HOA dues have been paid for the year, the buyer needs to reimburse the seller.

   Daily Rate: $800 ÷ 360 = $2.2222
   Buyer Days: Oct (0) + Nov (30) + Dec (30) = 60 days
   Buyer Charge: $2.2222 X 60 = $133.33 Debit Buyer / Credit Seller

2. B – Debit Buyer $40 / Debit Seller $260. The HOA dues in this problem are paid quarterly, so it is important to adjust to the time period, thus divide the quarterly HOA dues by 90. Since the HOA dues have not been paid and the attorney will pay the bill at closing, it is a double debit entry for different amounts.

Daily Rate: $300 ÷ 90 = $3.3333
Buyer Days: March 30 – 18 = 12
Buyer Charge: $3.3333 X 12 = $40
Seller Charge: $300 - $40 = $260
Entry: Debit Buyer $40 / Debit Seller $260

3. C – Debit Buyer $35 / Credit Seller $35. The HOA due are charged monthly so it is important to divide by 30. Since the HOA dues have been paid by the seller for the month, the buyer needs to reimburse the seller for the number of days that they own the property.

Daily Rate: $150 ÷ 30 = $5.00
Buyer Days: 30 – 23 = 7
Buyer Charge: $5.00 X 7 = $35 Debit Buyer / Credit Seller

MINI-CLOSING PROBLEMS – DUE FROM BUYER / NET TO SELLER

1. D - $111,750. When calculating the seller's net, the seller typically pays commission, deed prep and excise tax and the remainder are buyer's expenses (unless otherwise stated).

Sales Price	$200,000
Less Commission	-11,000 ($200,000 X 5.5%)
Less Deed Prep	-150
Less Excise Tax	-400 ($200,000 ÷ 500, round up)
Less Mortgage	-77,000
Add Tax	+300
Seller Net	$111,750

Property Tax
Days: N (15) + D (30) = 45 Days
Daily Rate: $2,400 ÷ 360 = $6.6667
Entry: $6.6667 X 45 = $300 – Debit Buyer / Credit Seller

2. B - $9,630. The seller pays commission, deed preparation and excise tax and therefore these can be ignored. Earnest money and due diligence fees are credited to the buyer as they are closing costs on the property.

Sales Price	$96,000
Less Loan	-86,400 ($96,000 X 90%)
Add Loan Orig	+1,296 ($86,400 X 1.5%)
Add Interim Int	+234 ($86,400 X 7.5% ÷ 360 X 13 Days)
Less EMD	-1,000
Less DDF	-500
Due from Buyer	$9,630

3. C - $19,990. The seller pays commission, deed preparation and excise tax and therefore these can be ignored. Since property taxes are not paid and closing is after September 1, the buyer and seller would be charged property tax for his/her respective amounts.

Sales Price	$285,000
Less Loan	-275,025 ($285,000 X 96.5%)
Add Interim Int	+487 ($275,025 X 3.75% ÷ 360 X 17 Days)
Add Survey	+400
Add Loan Orig	+2,750 ($275,000 X 1%)
Add Discount Pnts	+5,500 ($275,000 X 2%)
Add Appraisal	+350
Add Property Tax	+528
Due from Buyer	$19,990

   Property Tax
   Days: O (16) + ND (60) = 76 Days
   Daily Rate: $2,500 ÷ 360 = $6.9444
   Entry: $6.9444 X 76 = $527.78 – Debit Buyer

4. B - $207,472. The seller typically pays C, D an E – commission, deed preparation and excise tax. The remaining costs are typically paid by the buyer unless the problem states otherwise. Since closing is before September 1 and taxes are unpaid, calculate the seller's number of days, then debit the seller / credit the buyer.

Sales Price	$369,000
Less Commission	-22,140 ($369,000 X 6%)
Less Deed Prep	-250
Less Excise	-738 ($369,000 / 500, round up)
Less Loan Payoff	-135,950
Less Property Tax	-2,450
Net to Seller	$207,472

   Property Tax
   Days: JFMAMJ (180) + J (30) = 210
   Daily Rate: $4,200 ÷ 360 = $11.6666
   Entry: $11.6666 X 210 = $2,450

5. D - $25,968. The seller typically pays commission, deed preparation and excise tax so these items should be ignored when calculating the amount of money that the buyer will need to bring to closing. When calculating interim interest remember to add the day of closing as the bank is greedy and that interim/prepaid interest is calculated for only one month (the bank will find you for the remaining 360 payments). When a buyer purchase a property the earnest money deposit and due diligence fee are credited toward the purchase price.

Sales Price	$265,000
Less Loan	-238,000 ($265,000 X 90% LTV)
Add Origination fee	+2,385 ($238,000 X 1%)
Less Due Diligence	-1,000
Less Earnest Money	-2,500
Add Interim Interest	+538 ($238,000 X 5.5% ÷ 360 X 16 days)
Due from Buyer	$25,968

VALUATION – SALES COMPARISON APPROACH

1. B - $4,083. Appreciation is calculated based upon the comparable's sales price. It is typically given as a percentage for the year so you need to convert it to a monthly amount. You never adjust the subject property; only make adjustments to the comparable.

   Appreciation for year: $245,000 X 5% / 12 = $1,020.83
   Comp Appreciation: $1,020.83 X 4 = $4,083

2. D - $1,800,000. The front footage is the first call number when a lot is described, so this property has 200 front feet.

   Estimated market value: 200 X $9,000 = $1,800,000

3. A - $29,000. Never make adjustments to the subject property – only make adjustments to comparable properties. When the comp is superior – subtract; when a comp is inferior – increase.

   Square footage adjustment: 200 sqft. X $145 = $29,000. Comp superior – subtract.

4. C - $418,700. It is recommended that you list out the property features for the subject and comparable property before making adjustments. Two half baths do not equal a whole so make sure to separate them into full and half baths to avoid calculation errors. Comp Superior subtract (CSS) / Comp inferior Increase (CII)

Subject	Comparable	$400,000
3,400 sqft.	3,200 sqft	+20,000 (200 X 100) CII
4 BR	4 BR	No Adj
2 FB	3 FB	-2,800
1 HB	0 HB	+1,500
Deck	Deck	No Adj
	Probable SP	**$418,700**

5. D - $260,000. When no adjustments are given, you need to calculate them by comparing the comps provided. Comp 2 and Comp 3 are most similar except for square footage - $20,000 and 200 sqft – so the adjustment is $100 per sqft. Comp 1 and Comp 3 are most similar except for the fireplace – so a fireplace is worth $5,000.

Comp 1 - $250,000 + $10,000 sqft = $260,000
Comp 2 - $265,000 - $10,000 sqft + $5,000 FP = $260,000
Comp 3 - $245,000 + 10,000 sqft + $5,000 FP = $260,000

6. B - $183,000 - $192,000. When comp has negative features, it is inferior so increase/add. When a comp has positive features, it is superior so subtract.

   Comp A - $190,000 - $7,000 = $183,000
   Comp B - $187,000 + $5,000 = $192,000
   Comp C - $195,000 - $8,000 = $187,000

7. C - $183,400. When adjusting the comp, make sure that you are using the sales price not the list price.

Sales Price	175,000
+ Sqft	+ 4,250 (50 X $85 – inferior increase)
- Full Bath	- 4,000 (superior subtract)
+ Half Bath	+ 1,700 (inferior increase)
+ Deck	+ 3,500 (inferior increase)
+ Appr	+ 2,917 ($175,000 X 4% ÷ 12 X 5 m)

   Adj Probable SP $183,367, rounded to $183,400

VALUATION – COST APPROACH

1. D - $9,750. Depreciation is typically calculated using the straight line method. First calculate the cost to build the building new. Then divide the cost new by the useful life.

   Cost New: 5,000 sqft. X $195 = $975,000
   Straight-line Depreciation per year: $975,000 / 100 = $9,750

2. A - $500,000. Cost New / Useful Life = Straight-line Depreciation. To calculate the accumulated depreciation, take the straight-line depreciation per year and multiply by the effective age. The actual age is often given in cost approach problems as a distractor.

   Straight-line Depreciation: $2,500,000 / 75 = $33,333.33
   Depreciation: $33,333.33 X 15 = $500,000

3. C - $2,044,000. To calculate the probable sales price of a property using the cost approach, recall the formula: New – Depreciation + Land and Improvements.

   Building New: 15,000 sqft. X $175 = $2,625,000
   Depreciation: $2,625,000 / 80 X 20 = $656,250
   Probable Sales Price: $2,625,000 - $656,250 + 75,000 = $2,043,750, rounded $2,044,000

4. C - $645,000. When using the cost approach the actual age of the building is a distractor. You will need to calculate the value of the building new, back out depreciation and then add in the value of land and improvements.

   New: 4,000 X $150 = $600,000
   Depr: $600,000 ÷ 200 Useful X 15 Effective = $45,000
   Property Value: $600,000 - $45,000 Depr + $60,000 Land + $30,000 Improvements = $645,000

5. A - $3,549,000. Calculate the cost of the building new, then using useful or economic life determine the amount of straight-line depreciation per year. Next calculate the total depreciation by multiplying the per year amount by the effective age. Actual age is often a distractor.

   New: 25,000 X $145 = $3,625,000
   Depr: $3,625,000 ÷ 155 Useful X 15 Effective = $350,806
   Property Value: $3,625,000 - $350,806 Depr + $200,000 Land + $75,000 Improvements = $3,549,194, rounded

6. D - $1,149,000. Calculate the cost of the building new, then using useful or economic life determine the amount of straight-line depreciation per year. Next calculate the total depreciation by multiplying the per year amount by the effective age. Actual age is often a distractor.

   New: 4,500 X $200 = $900,000
   Depr: $900,000 ÷ 85 Useful X 10 Effective = $105,882
   Property Value: $900,000 - $105,882 Depr + $355,000 Land = $1,149,178, rounded

VALUATION – INCOME APPROACH – INCOME CAPITALIZATION

1. B – NOI/Value. It is important for testing purposes to memorize the steps used for math problems as you could be tested on the formula, what is included or excluded from the calculation, etc. It is recommended that you use the "T-bar" for income capitalization problems.

   Sales price ÷ annual rent = Gross Income Multiplier.
   Loan ÷ value = Loan to Value.
   Before-tax cash flow ÷ equity = cash-on-cash rate of return.

2. B - $1,363,000. It is important to know that depreciation, debt service and capital improvements are not considered operating expenses. We recommend that you write down the steps to calculate net operating income on your scrap paper before you start taking your exam. This will protect you against common distractors, although this problem is straight forward.

Gross Income	$400,000
- Vacancy & Collection	-16,000 ($400,000 X 4%)
= Effective Gross Inc.	$384,000 (**MOST COMMON DISTRACTOR**)
- Operating Expense	-275,000
= Net Operating Income	$109,000

   Value = NOI / Cap Rate = $109,000 / 8% = $1,362,500 – rounded $1,363,000

3. B - $125,000. Effective gross income is a common distractor. Note that it is calculated by taking gross income and subtracting vacancy and collection losses. Make sure to skip over gross income and vacancy and collection to ensure you avoid the common mistake of subtracting V&C again. Another name for effective gross income is total anticipated revenue.

Gross Income	
- Vacancy & Collection	
= Total Anticipated Rev.	$300,000 (**MOST COMMON DISTRACTOR**)
- Operating Expense	-175,000
= Net Operating Income	$125,000

4. A - $1,971,000. One of the biggest distractors in income capitalization problems is effective gross income. Effective Gross Income is calculated by taking gross income and subtracting vacancy and collection losses. Depreciation, debt service and capital improvements are not operating expenses.

Gross Income
-Vac & Coll
Eff. Gross Inc. $890,000
- Mgt Fee   - 89,000 ($890,000 X 10%)
- Other Oper   - 525,000
NOI $276,000

Value: $276,000 ÷ 14% = $1,971,429, rounded

5. A - $100,344. When calculating net operating income you do not include depreciation, debt service or capital improvements. Property taxes are considered an operating expense.

Gross Income $270,000 (15 X $1,500 X 12)
-Vac & Coll   - 16,200 ($270,000 X 6%)
Eff. Gross Inc. $253,800
- Mgt Fee   - 30,456 ($253,800 X 12%)
- Prop Tax   - 24,000
- Other Oper   - 99,000
NOI $100,344

6. A - $950,000. When performing this calculation, you can choose to back out the 2 units that will remain vacant or calculate as illustrated.

Gross Income $348,000 (20 X $1,450 X 12)
-Vac & Coll   - 37,700 [(2 X $1,450 X 12) + 2,900]
Eff. Gross Inc. $310,300
- Mgt Fee - 24,824 ($310,300 X 8%)
- Utilities - 55,000
- Prop Tax   - 60,000
- Other Oper   - 85,000
NOI $85,476

Value = $85,476 ÷ 9% = $949,733

VALUATION – GROSS RENT (INCOME) MULTIPLIER

1. A - 12. The gross income multiplier is calculated by taking the sales price and dividing by annual income.

   GIM: $2,100,000 / $75,000 = 12

2. A – $187,500. In this problem we have replaced sales price with estimate of market value. The estimated market value of a property using the gross rent multiplier is calculated by taking the monthly rent and multiplying by the GRM.

   Estimated market value: $750 X 250 = $187,500

3. C – 96. The gross rent multiplier is calculated by taking the sales price and dividing by monthly rent.

   Monthly Rent: $250,000 / 12 = $20,833
   GRM: $2,000,000 / $20,833 = 96

4. D - $4,375,000. There are two options to solving the problem – either making all rent monthly and calculate the GRM or make all income yearly and calculate the GIM to use with the property the investor is interested in purchasing. The capitalization rate is a distractor and not needed to solve the problem.

   Comp GIM: $3,750,000 ÷ $360,000 = 10.4167
   Comp GRM: $3,750,000 ÷ $30,000 = 125

   Value Subject GIM: $420,000 X 10.416666 = $4,375,000
   Value Subject GRM: $35,000 X 125 = $4,375,000

5. C – 150. The gross rent multiplier is calculated by taking the sales price and dividing it by monthly rent. Note that the property is a duplex that rents for $2,700 per unit, meaning that monthly rent is $5,400.

   GRM: $810,000 ÷ $5,400 = 150

6. A – 9.8333. The gross income multiplier is calculated by taking the sales price and dividing it by annual income. Not the property is a triplex that rents for $2,100 per unit, meaning annual income is $75,600.

   GIM: $743,400 ÷ $75,600 = 9.8333

GAIN ON SALE – PERCENTAGE

1. B – 19%. When calculating gain on the sale, make sure that you are using the sold price and not the list price. Calculate the change then divide it by the old/purchase price.

   Purchase Price: $105,000 X 80% = $84,000
   Gain: $100,000 – $84,000 = $16,000
   Percentage Gain: $16,000 ÷ $84,000 = 19%

2. B – 10%. When calculating the gain on sale, make sure that you are using the sold price and not the list price. (New-OLD) ÷ OLD.

   Gain: $412,500 – $375,000 = $37,500
   Percentage Gain: $37,500 ÷ $375,000 = 10%

PERCENTAGE GAIN ON EQUITY

1. D – 820%. In order to calculate the answer to this problem you need to know the amount of the initial loan as well as the amount of the down payment (initial equity). Next you will need to calculate the current fair market value of the property as well as well as the current loan balance. With that information you can calculate the current equity (FMV – loan balance). To calculate equity increase – (New – Old) / Old.

   Loan Amount: $650,000 - $50,000 = $600,000
   Initial Equity: Down Payment $50,000

   Appreciation: $650,000 X 40% = $260,000
   FMV: $650,000 + $260,000 = $910,000
   Loan Decrease: $600,000 X 25% = $150,000
   New Loan Balance: $600,000 - $150,000 = $450,000

New Equity: $910,000 - $450,000 = $460,000
Percentage Gain: ($460,000 -$50,000) / $50,000 = 8.2 or 820%

2. C – 189%. To solve this problem you need to know the original purchase price, loan amount and equity. Then calculate the current fair market value, current loan amount and new equity. To calculate equity increase – (New – Old) / Old. For this solution we will illustrate how you can skip a few steps to get to the answer faster. If you are not comfortable with this, solve with the same steps above. An 85% LTV requires a 15% down payment. If a loan decreased by 12%, then the new balance is 88% of the original amount borrowed.

   Original Equity: $425,000 X 15% = $63,750 (down payment)
   Original Loan: $425,000 - $63,750 = $361,250
   FMV: $425,000 X 1.18 = $501,500
   New Loan Balance: $361,250 X 88% = $317,900
   New Equity: $501,500 - $317,900 = $183,600
   Percentage Gain: ($183,600 - $63,500) / $63,500 = 1.89 or 189%

PROPERTY MANAGEMENT FEE

1. C – $38,412. Effective gross income is calculated when you take gross income and subtract out vacancy & collection losses. Effective gross income may also be called total anticipated revenue

   Gross Rent: $1,200 X 12 X 12 = $216,000
   $1,500 X 10 X 12 = $180,000
   $216,000 + $180,000 = $396,000
   Vacancy & Collection: $396,000 X 3% = $11,880
   EGI / TAR: $396,000 - $11,800 = $384,120
   Management Fee: $384,120 X 10% = $38,412

2. B – $432. The property is a duplex which means 2 units. It is a common mistake of license candidates to forget to multiply monthly rent per unit by the number of units that the property has. The rent was fully paid so there is no reason to back out V&C for this month,

   Gross Rent: $1,800 X 2 = $3,600
   Management Fee: $3,600 X 12% = $432

3. A - $110,100.

   Gross Rent: 100 X $1,250 X 12 = $1,500,000
   Vacancy & Collection Loss: (8 X $1,250 X 12) + $3,750 = $123,750
   Effective Gross Income: $1,500,000 - $123,750 = $1,376,250
   Management Fee: $1,376,250 X 8% = $110,100

PERCENTAGE LEASE – TOTAL RENT CALCULATION

1. C – $30,400. When calculating the total rent, you need to first calculate base rent and then the additional rent based upon sales.

   Base Rent: $1,200 X 12 = $14,400
   Percentage: ($900,000 - $500,000) X 4% = $16,000
   Total Rent: $14,400 + $16,000 = $30,400

2. C – $29,250. Rent for commercial space is typically quoted as an annual rate per square foot. To determine the base rate, multiply the per foot price X square footage.

   Base Rent: $15 X 1,400 sqft = $21,000
   Percentage: ($500,000 - $350,000) X 5.5% = $8,250
   Total Rent: $21,000 + $8,250 = $29,250

2. D - $50,000.

   Base Rent: $12 X 2,500 sqft = $30,000
   Percentage: ($950,000 - $450,000) X 4% = $20,000
   Total Rent: $30,000 + $20,000 = $50,000

End Solution

Math Practice Test 1

1. A provisional broker is representing a buyer in the purchase of a new home located at 1423 Pleasant Street. The home is listed for $129,900, however the buyer and seller agreed to $125,000. The listing agreement with the seller calls for 6% commission, with the seller's agent receiving 2.5% and selling agent 3.5%. How much will the selling agent receive if they split commission with his/her brokerage on a 70/30 basis, rounded to the nearest dollar?

   A. $3,063
   B. $3,248
   C. $4,375
   D. $4,547

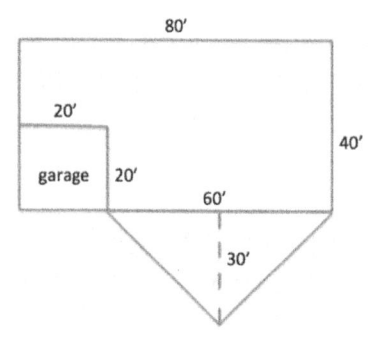

2. Based upon the illustration above, what is square footage of the living area for this single story home?

   A. 3,200
   B. 3,700
   C. 4,100
   D. 4,600

3. A property located in North Carolina is listed for $425,000 – has a sales price of $420,000 - a tax value of $380,000 – and an initial mortgage of $336,000. How much excise tax will be paid at closing if the tax is charged $1 per $500?

   A. $672
   B. $760
   C. $840
   D. $850

4. A buyer is purchasing a home for $200,000 with an 80% LTV at 4.75%. Annual property tax and insurance costs $2,700 and the mortgage factor is 5.21. The property is an owner occupied duplex that will rent for $1,200 per month. Assuming the buyer obtains a conventional loan and other recurring debt is $450 per month, what is the minimum monthly income necessary for borrower to qualify, rounded to the nearest dollar?

    A. $ 3,781
    B. $ 3,810
    C. $ 4,191
    D. $ 4,314

5. A seller has agreed to pay 6% commission on the first million dollars of sales price, 5% on the second million and 4% on the remainder. How much will the seller pay in total commission if the sales price is $4,800,000?

    A. $ 60,000
    B. $111,000
    C. $112,000
    D. $222,000

6. Sarah purchases a property located in the city for $345,000 and promptly builds an addition that cost $55,000. The assessed value on the property on the date of purchase was $310,000. What is the annual tax liability for the current year if the city tax rate is $0.45 and count tax rate is $0.90 if the property is located in North Carolina?

    A. $ 1,395
    B. $ 4,185
    C. $ 4,658
    D. $ 4,928

7. Alec purchased a lot two years ago that measures 400' X 350'. He recently purchased an adjoining lot that measures 77,800 square feet. How much is the combined property worth if comparable property sells for $75,000 per acre?

   A. $ 150,000
   B. $ 225,000
   C. $ 375,000
   D. $ 450,000

8. The seller wants to net $25,000 from the sale of his home. What would the selling price need to be if the loan payoff is $145,000 with the seller paying $3,000 in closing costs and commission at 6%, rounded to the nearest $100?

   A. $ 180,200
   B. $ 180,900
   C. $ 183,400
   D. $ 184,000

9. Eric is selling a home for $380,000 that is subject to a homeowner association with annual dues of $1,200. He agreed to pay 5.5% commission and $3,000 towards the buyer's closing costs. If closing is held April 19th and association dues have been paid for the year, what entry will be made on the closing worksheet for homeowner association dues, rounded to the nearest dollar if the seller pays the day of closing?

   A. Charge the buyer $837, Credit the seller $837.
   B. Charge the buyer $837
   C. Charge the buyer $363, Credit the seller $363
   D. Charge the buyer $363

10. A buyer is considering loan options in the purchase of their new home with a sales price of $180,000. The first lender is offering a 30-year mortgage with 5% down payment at 5.75% interest with a factor of 5.48. The second lender is offering a 15-year mortgage with a 5% down payment at 5.25% interest with a factor of 8.04. Both loans charge an origination fee of 1%. What is the difference in the amount of total interest that would be charged over the life of the two loans rounded to the nearest dollar?

   A. $89,878
   B. $94,608
   C. $192,375
   D. $202,500

11. An appraiser is working to calculate the appropriate estimate of value for a residential property based on 3 recently sold comparable properties. Based on the information shown below what is the indicated estimate of value?

Subject	Comp #1 – $245,000	Comp#2 - $240,000	Comp#3 - $235,000
2,300 sq. ft.	2,400 sq. ft.	2400 sq. ft.	2,300 sq. ft.
3 Bedroom	3 Bedroom	3 Bedroom	3 Bedroom
No Deck	Deck	No Deck	Deck

   A. $230,000
   B. $235,000
   C. $240,000
   D. $250,000

12. A buyer has annual income $111,000 and is applying for a 25-year conventional mortgage with principal and interest payments of $1,804 per month and $231 per month for taxes and insurance. The lender uses traditional loan qualifying ratios for a conventional mortgage. What is the maximum amount the buyer will be able to have in recurring long-term non-housing expenses?

   A. $ 555
   B. $ 740
   C. $1,193
   D. $1,295

13. An appraiser is calculating the value of a 40-unit apartment building. 30 of the units rent for $1,200 per month and 10 of the units rent for $1,400 per month. Vacancy and collection losses are 6% of gross potential income. The owner depreciated $40,000 last year on his tax return, paid $60,000 management fee and $90,000 in other annual operating expenses. What is the value of the building if the appropriate capitalization rate is 12%, rounded to the nearest thousand?

A. $1,801,000
B. $2,134,000
C. $3,117,000
D. $3,450,000

14. A buyer is purchasing a home with a monthly PI payment of $4,350, property taxes of $6,600 for the year and insurance is $2,400 per year. The bank requires escrowed funds for taxes and insurance. The borrower has recurring debt of $1,602 per month and the bank uses a 28/36 ratio. What is the minimum yearly income necessary for the borrower to qualify rounded to the nearest $100?

A. $ 18,200
B. $ 18,600
C. $218,600
D. $223,400

15. A broker is performing a broker price opinion on a 1,800 square foot home. The broker identified 3 similar properties that sold in the past year. Appreciation for the neighborhood as been at 5% per year. Comparable 1 has 1,900 square feet and sold for $195,000 three months ago. Comparable 2 has 1,750 square feet and sold for $181,000 five months ago. Comparable 3 has 1,850 square feet and sold for $184,500 nine months ago. The market indicates that an appropriate square footage value is $85 per square foot. What is the indicated range of value for the subject house, rounded to the nearest hundred?

A. $185,200 - $196,700
B. $187,200 - $189,000
C. $188,900 - $195,700
D. $189,000 - $195,700

16. A buyer is purchasing a home for $325,000 with an FHA loan requiring a 5% down payment at an interest rate of 5.25%. They paid $2,000 earnest money deposit and $500 due diligence fee. The property has annual property taxes of $4,800 are unpaid and will be paid by the attorney at closing. The closing is scheduled October 27th. The annual property insurance premium of $750 was paid outside of closing. The lender will collect interim interest and 3 months of taxes and insurance to fund the escrow account. What will buyer need to bring to closing, rounded to the nearest whole dollar if the seller pays taxes the day of closing?

A. $16,113
B. $16,158
C. $16,170
D. $16,908

17. John is interested in purchasing a triplex property that has a low vacancy and collection loss of 3%, which is listed for $475,000. John's broker, Maia, has found a comparable triplex that rent for $800 per unit that recently sold for $480,000. What is the gross income multiplier indicated by the comparable property?

A. 16.49
B. 16.67
C. 200.0
D. 600.0

18. A buyer obtains a mortgage loan of $335,000 on the purchase of a home that cost $350,000. The loan is for 30 years at an interest rate of 6.0% interest, with principal and interest payments of $6.010 per thousand dollars borrowed. What is the principal balance of the loan after the buyer makes one payment, rounded to the nearest dollar?

A. $334,662
B. $334,752
C. $349,647
D. $349,662

19. An apartment complex has an effective gross income of $1,250,000 per year with 6% vacancy and collection loss. The apartment complex has the following expenses:

Real Property Taxes	$45,000
Repair Reserves	$75,000
Other Operating Expenses	$405,000
Depreciation	$95,000
Debt Service	$350,000

An appraiser has determined through an evaluation of recently sold comparable properties that the capitalization rate is 14%. What is the estimate of value for the property, rounded to the nearest thousand?

A. $2,679,000
B. $4,500,000
C. $4,643,000
D. $5,179,000

20. A seller has decided to list his property for sale with a licensed broker. The broker is asked to calculate the estimated seller net proceeds for 3 potential sale prices. The seller has agreed to pay 6% commission on the gross sales price. The following expenses were paid by the seller:

Seller Closing Costs	1% of gross sales price
Deed Preparation	$ 200
Mortgage Payoff	$101,700
Sales Price 1	$250,000
Sales Price 2	$265,000
Sales Price 3	$245,000

What is the seller's net proceeds range based on the above information?

A. $125,950 - $144,550
B. $125,950 - $130,600
C. $130,600 - $144,550
D. $144,550 - $145,600

21. A property is under contract for $288,000 and is scheduled to close on September 26th. The buyer paid a $2,000 earnest money deposit and $1,000 due diligence fee. The buyer obtained a 90% LTV conventional mortgage at a fixed rate of 5.75% with the payment of 1% origination and 1 discount point. The seller's loan payoff on the date of closing is $114,700. Property taxes are $3,450 for the year and are unpaid, however will be charged to the respective parties and paid by the attorney at closing. The following closing expenses were paid by the respective parties in accordance with stand practice:

- Interim interest
- Deed Preparation $150
- Mortgage Satisfaction $15
- Title Insurance $450
- Excise Tax – North Carolina Standard
- Commission 7%

What is the net due to seller, rounded to the nearest dollar?

A. $ 35,542
B. $146,850
C. $148,850
D. $150,500

22. Patty purchased a property for $145,000 in a desirable neighborhood 10 years ago. She listed the property at $500,000 and it sold where net proceeds were $480,000. What is her percentage profit from the sale?

A. 29%
B. 30%
C. 231%
D. 245%

23. A borrower obtains a 30-year fixed rate VA loan with a 5.25% interest rate. The purchase price of the home is $168,000 with a 3% down payment. The closing is scheduled for December 17th. What is the interim/prepaid interest to be charged to the borrower on the Closing Disclosure, rounded to the nearest dollar?

A. $309
B. $319
C. $333
D. $343

24. The assessed value of a property is $450,000. The property is located in North Carolina in the county only. Local ad valorem taxes are charged at $0.95 per $100 of assessed value for property located in the county and $1.95 per $100 of assessed value for property located in the city. Closing is scheduled for September 29th and the seller has paid for the entire year. What is the tax proration between the buyer and seller if the seller pays the day of closing?

   A. Credit seller $1,080.63 and Charge buyer $1,080.63
   B. Charge seller $1,080.63 and Credit buyer $1,080.63
   C. Credit seller $2,218.13 and Charge buyer $2,218.13
   D. Charge seller $2,218.13 and Credit buyer $2,218.13

25. A duplex rents for $13,800 annually per unit. It recently sold for $496,800. What is the Gross Rent Multiplier?

   A. 18
   B. 36
   C. 136
   D. 216

Math Practice Test 1 - Solution

1. A - $3,063. Commission is based upon the sales price of the home. The selling agent is the agent that represents the buyer. The seller's agent would be the listing agent.

   Sales Price $125,000 X 3.5% = $4,375
   $4,375 X 70% = $3,062.50, then round up to $3,063

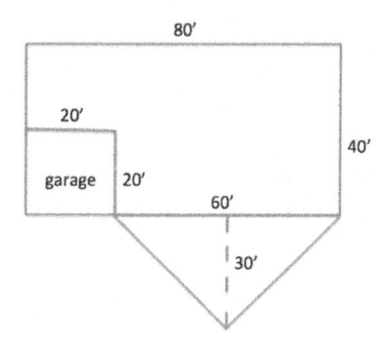

   [Diagram: Floor plan showing an 80' x 40' rectangle with a 20' x 20' garage cut out on the left side, and a triangle extending below with base 60' and height 30']

2. B – 3,700 square feet. Living area must be Heated, Finished and Directly Accessible. One way to remember this is "Happy Feet Dance Always". Therefore, the garage will not be included in the square footage. The area of a triangle is calculated as ½ Base X Height

   Large Rectangle: 80' X 40' = 3,200
   Less Garage: 20' X 20' = -400
   Add Triangle: ½ 60' X 30' = 900

   Living Area: 3,200 – 400 + 900 = 3,700

3. C - $840. Excise tax is paid by the seller at closing unless otherwise stated and is paid at $1 per $500 of sales price. To calculate take the Sales Price / $500 and round up to the next whole dollar.

   Sales Price $420,000 / 500 = $840

4. C - $4,191. First you must calculate the PITI payment and Total Long-term debt payments. The rent is a distractor and is not used to solve for the minimum income necessary to qualify. Recall that the minimum income is the HIGHER of the two monthly income amounts. Also, before solving the problem make sure that you are solving for the correct amount; the question may call for monthly or yearly income needed.

    If the monthly payment is not provided, you may need to use a factor or amortization rate to determine the Principal & Interest payment.

    First Calculate the PITI Payment:

    $200,000 PP x 80% LTV = $160,000
    $160,000 ÷ 1,000 = 160
    160 X Factor 5.21 = Monthly P&I $833.60
    Yearly Tax & Ins. $2,700 ÷ 12 = $225.00
    PITI Payment: $833.60 + $225.00 = $1,058.60

    Total Debt: PITI $1,058.60 + $450 = $1,508.60

    Housing $1,058.60 ÷ 28% = $3,780.71
    Total Debt $1,508.60 ÷ 36% = $4,190.55

5. D - $222,000. A listing agreement may call for tiered commission to be paid. Follow the instructions for each tier.

    Tier 1 Commission: $1,000,000 X 6% = $60,000
    Tier 2 Commission: $1,000,000 X 5% = $50,000
    Tier 3 Sales Price: $4,800,000 - $2,000,000 = $2,800,000
    Tier 3 Commission: $2,800,000 X 4% = $112,000

    Total Commission: $60,000 + $50,000 + $112,000 = $222,000

6. B - $4,185. In North Carolina property tax rates are expressed as a dollar amount per $100 of assessed value. The property taxes attach on January 1 and therefore any additions will impact the following years tax value. In addition, the assessed value does not change in North Carolina when the property is sold, only when the values are reassessed which could be every year, but must occur every 8 years. Since the property is located in the city, Sarah will pay both city and county taxes. If the property were located in the county, but not in the city, then only county taxes would have been paid.

    $310,000 Assessed Value ÷ $100 = 3,100
    3,100 X $1.35 = $4,185

7. C - $375,000. First you must calculate the total square footage of the two lots. Then divide this by 43,560 (square footage in an acre). Take the acreage and multiply it by the price per acre to get a projected value for the lot based on the sale of a similar property

    Lot 1: 400' X 350' = 140,000 sqft
    Lot 2: 77,800
    Total Square Footage: 140,000 + 77,800 = 217,800
    217,800 ÷ 43,560 = 5 acres
    5 acres X $75,000 = $375,000

8. D - $184,000. First add up the known seller expenses and amount that the seller wants to net. The only amount not known is the amount of commission the seller will pay. This number represents the needed amount to cover everything except commission, including the amount the seller wants to net. It is important to note that the commission is paid off of the sales price, which we are calculating, not on the lower amount.

    Net $25,000 + Payoff $145,000 + Closing Cost $3,000 = $173,000

    Next we calculate the percentage of proceeds remaining after commission. So if the Sales Price is 100% and Commission is 6%, then the remainder is 94%.

    $173,000 ÷ 94% = $184,042, rounded to $184,000

    Most errors occur when a student takes the known expenses and adds 6% to this amount. Ask yourself, do I want to earn 6% of $173,000 or 6% of $184,000. Perhaps this will help us avoid this error.

9. A – Debit Buyer $837 / Credit Seller $837. This is a basic proration of expenses and in similar to calculating the proration of taxes. Be careful when answering these questions as it could state that the buyer or the seller will pay the day of closing. Since the dues have been paid for the year by the seller, we must charge the buyer for the days they will on the property (debit) and reimburse the seller (credit).

    First calculate the dues per day: $1,200 ÷ 360 = $3.3333

    Next calculate the buyer's number of days: (Apr) 11 + (May-Dec) 240 = 251 days

    251 Days X $3.3333 = $836.67

10. A - $89,878. In order to calculate the total amount of interest paid you must take the monthly principal and interest payment and multiply it by the number of payments (30 year – 360 payments / 15 year – 180 payments). This will give the total principal and interest paid over the life of the loan. When a problem, like this one, calls for the comparison of two loans and the amount borrowed is the same, then there is no need to back out the principal amount borrowed.

    First calculate the loan amount: $180,000 X 95% = $171,000
    Recall that factors or amortization rates are monthly payments per $1,000 borrowed.

    30 Year Loan – P&I Payment: $171,000 ÷ 1,000 = 171 X Factor 5.48 = $937.08
    Total P&I: $937.08 X 360 = $337,349

    15 Year Loan – P&I Payment: $171,000 ÷ 1,000 = 171 X Factor 8.04 = $1,374.84
    Total P&I: $1,374.84 X 180 = $247,471

    Total Interest Difference: $337,349 - $247,471 = $89,878

11. A - $230,000. When adjustments are not provided in the problem, the first step is to determine how much something is worth. Looking at the Comps in this example two are very similar except for square footage (comp #1 and comp #3) with relation to square footage. The difference in sales price is $10,000 and square footage of 100 square feet. By dividing $10,000 by 100 we can calculate the value of square footage as $100 per square foot. Similarly, two comps are very similar except for the deck (comp #1 and comp #2). The difference in sales price is $5,000, so that is the adjustment for the deck.

    Adjustments as follows:

Subject	Comp #1 – $245,000	Comp#2 - $240,000	Comp#3 - $235,000
2,300 sq. ft.	2,400 sq. ft. -10,000	2400 sq. ft. – 10,000	2,300 sq. ft. No Adj.
3 Bedroom	3 Bedroom No Adj.	3 Bedroom No Adj.	3 Bedroom No Adj.
No Deck	Deck -5,000	No Deck No Adj.	Deck -5,000
ADJ Sales Price	$230,000	$230,000	$230,000

12. D - $1,295. Generally, with qualifying problems you calculate both ratios. It is not necessary to calculate the housing ratio as the problem is asking for the maximum amount of long term non-housing debt the borrower can carry and still qualify for the mortgage.

Annual Income $111,000 ÷ 12 = $9,250
$9,250 X 36% = $3,330 Max Total Debt
$3,330 – PITI $2,035 = $1,295

13. D - $3,450,000. When using the direct capitalization method or income capitalization method, the value = net operating income ÷ cap rate. The first step is to calculate NOI by taking Gross Income – Vacancy & Collection = Effective Gross Income – Operating Expenses = NOI. We recommend that you always write out the equation so that you do not make the mistake of backing out vacancy and collection from effective gross income when that has been provided. Effective Gross Income may also be referred to as Total Anticipated Revenue.

    Gross Income: 30 X 1,200 X 12 = $432,000
                   10 X 1,400 X 12 = $168,000
                   Total Gross Income $600,000
    Vacancy & Collection: $600,000 X 6% = $36,000

    GI $600,000 – V&C $36,000 - $60,000 MGT Fee - $90,000 Op Exp = NOI $414,000
    $414,000 ÷ 12% = $3,450,000

14. D - $223,400. When you are working with minimum income to qualifying problems always double check if you are calculating monthly or yearly amounts. Break out the payments between Housing Debt and Total Debt, then divide by 28% and 36% respectively. The problem calls for yearly income so then multiply the highest number by 12.

    Housing Debt: $4,350P&I + $750T&I = $5,100 PITI
    Monthly T&I: ($6,600 + $2,400) ÷ 12 = $750
    $5,100 ÷ 28% = $18,214 X 12 = $218,571

    Total Debt: $5,100 PITI + $1,602 LT Debt = $6,702
    $6,702 ÷ 36% = $18,617 X 12 = $223,404

15. B - $187,200 - $189,000. It is important to remember that we only adjust the comparable properties. Comp Superior = Subtract / Comp Inferior = Increase. When calculating appreciation take the Comp SP X Appr Rate ÷ 12 X # of months since sale.

    Comp 1: SP $195,000 - $8,500 SQFT ADJ + $2,437.50 APPR = $188,937.50
    SQFT ADJ: 100 SQFT X $85 = $8,500 Superior Subtract
    APPR ADJ: $195,000 X 5% ÷ 12 X 3 = $2,347.50

Comp 2: SP $181,000 + $4,250 SQFT ADJ + $3,770.83 APPR = $189,020.50
SQFT ADJ: 50 SQFT X $85 = $4,250 Inferior Increase
APPR ADJ: $181,000 X 5% ÷ 12 X 5 = $3,770.83

Comp 3: SP $184,500 - $4,250 SQFT ADJ + $6,918.75 = $187,168.75
SQFT ADJ: 50 SQFT X $85 = $4,250 Superior Subtract
APPR ADJ: $184,500 X 5% ÷ 12 X 9 = $6,918.75

16. B - $16,158. Make sure to check which party will be paying taxes the day of closing. In some national problems the buyer will pay the day of closing so you will treat it similar to the calculation of interim interest by adding a day to the buyer. In North Carolina, the seller typically pays the day of closing.

    $325,000.00 Purchase Price
    - $308,750.00 Loan ($325,000 X 95% LTV)
    - $ 2,000.00 EMD
    - $ 500.00 DDF
    +$ 840.00 Taxes ($4800 ÷ 360 = 13.3333 X 63 Days) (O) 3 + (ND) 60 = 63 days
    +$ 180.10 Int. Int. ($308,750 X 5.25% = $16,209.37 ÷ 360 = $45.0260
                     $45.0260 X 4 Days = $180.10) Days: 30 – 27 +1 = 4 Days
    +$ 187.50 Ins. Esc. ($750 ÷ 12 X 3 months)
    +$ 1,200.00 Tax Esc. ($4,800 ÷ 12 X 3)
     $ 16,157.60

17. B – 16.67. The multiplier will be expressed as either Gross Income Multiplier or Gross Rent Multiplier. Gross Income is based on annual income, while gross rent is based on monthly rent. Another item to be cautious of is the number of units and how rent is expressed. To calculate the Gross Income Multiplier you would take the Sales Price and ÷ Gross Income.

    Gross Income: $800 X 3units X 12 months = $28,800
    Gross Income Multiplier: $480,000 SP ÷ $28,800 GI = 16.667

18. A - $334,662. To determine the principal balance after one payment you need to be able to split the monthly P&I payment into the principal and interest components. To do this you must calculate the amount of money paid that month towards interest.

    P&I Payment: $335,000 ÷ 1,000 X 6.010 Factor = $2,013.35
    Monthly Interest: $335,000 X 6% ÷ 12 = $1,675
    Principal Payment: $2,013.35 - $1,675 = $338.35
    New Balance: $335,000 - $338.35 = $334,662

19. D - $5,179,000. In order to determine the value of a property using the direct capitalization method you must remember the formula: Value = NOI ÷ Cap Rate. In addition recall that NOI = GI – V&C = EGI – Op Exp = NOI (no depreciation, debt service or capital improvements).

    NOI = GI – V&C = $1,250,000 - $45,000 Prop Tax - $75,000 Rep Res - $405,000 Other Op Exp = $725,000

    NOI $725,000 ÷ Cap Rate 14% = $5,178,571 rounded to $5,179,000

20. A - $125,950 - $144,550. With this problem you will need to make 3 separate calculations similar to the sales comparison approach, where you provide a range.

    Seller Net Sale 1: $250,000 – Comm 6% (15,000) – C/C 1% (2,500) – 200 Deed – Loan Payoff 101,700 = $130,600

    Seller Net Sale 2: $265,000 – Comm 6% (15,900) – C/C 1% (2,650) – 200 Deed – Loan Payoff 101,700 = $144,550

    Seller Net Sale 3: $245,000 – Comm 6% (14,700) – C/C 1% (2,450) – 200 Deed – Loan Payoff 101,700 = $125,950

21. C - $148,850. The first step is to determine who's net you calculating, which in this case is the seller. The seller typically pays commission, deed prep and excise tax. Recall that the due diligence fee has already been paid to the seller and therefore must be charged to them as the buyer will be credited this amount. In addition, this problem contains a mortgage satisfaction fee which would be paid by the seller.

    Sales Price $288,000
    - LOAN $114,700
    - DDF $ 1,000
    - Tax $ 2,549
    - Deed Prep $ 150
    - Mtg Sat $ 15
    - Excise Tax $ 576
    - Comm. $ 20,160
    Net Seller $148,850

22. C – 231%. First calculate the amount of the gain by taking Sales Proceeds less the original purchase price. Then take the difference and divide it by the original purchase price for the percentage change.

    $480,000 Proceeds – $145,000 Purchase Price = $335,000
    $335,000 ÷ $145,000 = 2.31 or 231%

23. C - $333. You first need to calculate the amount of the loan and multiply it by te interest rate to get interest for the year. Divide yearly interest by 360 to calculate the daily rate. Next calculate the number of days. Multiply the daily rate by the number of days.

    Loan Amount: $168,000 Purchase Price X 97% LTV = $162,960
    Yearly Interest: $162,960 X 5.25% = $8,555.40
    Daily Interest: $8,555.40 ÷ 360 = $23.765
    Number of Days: 30 – 17 + 1 = 14 Days
    Entry: $23.765 X 14 days = $332.71 rounded to $333

24. A – Credit Seller / Debit Buyer $1,080.63. To calculate taxes for the year in North Carolina take the assessed value ÷ 100 X tax rate. To prorate the taxes you must calculate the daily rate by taking the tax for the year and ÷ 360. Next you must determine the number of days, in this question for the buyer. Then multiply the daily rate by the number of days. When taxes were paid by the seller for the year, the buyer must give money back to the seller, so debit or charge the buyer / credit seller.

    Tax for Year: ($450,000 ÷ 100) X $0.95 = $4,275
    Daily Rate: $4,275 ÷ 360 = 11.875
    Buyer Days: (S) 1 + (OND) 90 = 91 Days
    Prorated Taxes: $11.875 X 91 = $1,080.63

25. D – 216. In order to calculate the Gross Rent Multiplier you need to remember the formula Sales Price ÷ Monthly Rent. Make sure to carefully read the problem for the number of units, in this problem a duplex.

    Total Rent per year: $13,800 X 2 Units = $27,600
    Rent per Month: $27,600 ÷12 = $2,300
    Gross Rent Multiplier: Sales Price $496,800 ÷ $2,300 = 216

End Solutions

Math Practice Test 2

1. A couple is interested in purchasing a house in Winston-Salem. The husband makes $50,000 annually and his wife makes $60,000 per year. The lender is qualifying the couple using a conventional loan with a 20% down payment and 28%/36% ratios. The couple also has two car loans totaling $630 per month and one student loan of $250 per month. What is the maximum housing expense for which the couple qualifies?

   A. $2,420
   B. $2,494
   C. $2,567
   D. $3,300

2. A homebuyer recently located a house that he is interested in purchasing. To finance the house, the debt service would total $925 a month and the taxes and insurance would average $250 per month and his other debts total $580. What is the minimum income necessary to qualify for a loan on this property if the lender uses qualifying ratios of 28%/36%?

   A. $3,264
   B. $4,196
   C. $4,535
   D. $4,875

3. A buyer is contemplating financing a property and has received the following information from his lender: a 30-year fixed loan with an interest rate of 4.25% on his $250,000 mortgage would cost him $1,229.85 in principal and interest. However, he may receive an interest rate of 3.75% on a 15-year mortgage with a monthly debt service of $1,818.05. How much will the buyer save over the life of the loan if he opts for the 15-year loan?

   A. $ 77,249
   B. $115,497
   C. $192,756
   D. $327,249

4. A purchaser inquires of her agent as to how much she will need to be prepared to bring to closing. The agent notes that the purchase price of the home is $185,000 and the lender requires a 20% down payment. The lender is also charging one discount point and $585 for loan origination on the buyer's loan at 5% for 30 years. Interim interest will also be paid for the end of the month on the April 23rd closing date. The real property taxes are $1,026 for the year. Homeowner's insurance is $600 for the year and will be collected at closing. A credit report of $50 and an appraisal fee of $300 were paid at the time of loan application The agents' commissions are 6% of the total sale price and excise taxes are to be charged at the state rate. The closing attorney charges $725 for closings and the lender's title insurance is $370. At the time of the contract, the buyer paid a $200 due diligence fee and a $2,000 earnest money deposit. How much will the buyer need to bring to closing in this scenario?

A. $32,237.95
B. $37,802.39
C. $38,402.39
D. $38,752.39

5. An appraiser is valuing a unique commercial property and has determined the following: the building would cost $300 per square foot to build today using standard construction methods and it measures 3,500 square feet. Buildings of this nature have an economic life of approximately 60 years and this particular building has an effective age of 15 years. The lot on which the building sits has a value of $250,000 in the current market. What is the value of this property using the cost approach?

A. $ 762,500
B. $1,050,000
C. $1,037,500
D. $1,550,000

6. A seller is trying to determine whether it is the right time to sell his property. He would like to net $50,000 after selling the house and paying all of his obligations. For what price must he sell the property to accomplish his goal, after paying off his mortgage of $175,000, his estimated closing costs of $2,500 and a 6% commission to his agent, rounded to the nearest hundred?

A. $227,500
B. $241,200
C. $241,900
D. $242,000

7. An agent is performing a CMA on a subject property that has three bedrooms and 2 baths, 2,000 square feet, and a one car garage. The subject property also has a fireplace, no patio, and recent upgrades worth $15,000. The agent has located a comparable property which sold for $190,000 three months earlier and has the following characteristics: 3 bedrooms and a bath and a half, 2,050 square feet, a one car garage, a patio, no fireplace, and no significant upgrades. Contribution values for the area are $25 per square foot, $2,500 for a full bath and $1,500 for a half bath, $7,000 for a one car garage, $1,000 for a fireplace, $4,000 for a patio, and appreciation has average 3% per year in this neighborhood. What is the indicated value of the subject property?

A. $188,175
B. $201,750
C. $203,175
D. $203,675

8. A property owner is attempting to sell his property for $225,000. He had previously purchased the property for $175,000. What will the owner's percent of profit be if he sells for his asking price?

A. 22.2%
B. 28.6%
C. 72.4%
D. 77.8%

9. An investor is researching the purchase of a single family home to be used as a residential rental. In the neighborhood where the property is located, similar houses sell for $150,000. These houses are able to command a rent of $1,250 per month. What would be a reasonable gross monthly rent multiplier in this neighborhood?

A. 10
B. 120
C. 125
D. 150

10. A buyer purchase a home by assuming the VA loan on the property. On the first of the month, the veteran's loan balance was $140,000 and the interest rate was 3.5% and the closing occurred on June 12th. How would the assumed interest appear on the closing disclosure?

   A. $163.33 Debit Seller, $163.33 Credit Buyer
   B. $245.00 Debit Seller, $250.00 Credit Buyer
   C. $250.00 Debit Seller, $163.33 Debit Buyer
   D. $250.00 Debit Buyer

11. A homeowner currently has a loan balance of $245,000 and an interest rate of 4%. His current PITI payment is $1,470, of which $300 goes to taxes and insurance. What will be the homeowner's loan balance after his next monthly payment, rounded to the nearest dollar?

   A. $243,530
   B. $243,830
   C. $244,347
   D. $244,647

12. A buyer has located a property that will require a housing expense of $1,800. He currently has an annual income of $84,000 per year and expenses other than housing of $800. Under which of the following ratios will the buyer qualify under conventional loan ratios?

   A. The maximum total debt allowed is $2,520 and the buyer qualifies for the loan.
   B. The maximum housing payment is $1,960 and the buyer does not qualify for the loan.
   C. The maximum housing payment is $2,520 and the buyer qualifies for the loan.
   D. The maximum total debt payment is $1,960 and the buyer does not qualify for the loan.

13. How would the rent proration appear on the closing disclosure if an investor is purchasing a property with a tenant in place with a monthly rent of $1,300 and the closing is taking place on March 24, assuming that rent has been paid for the month (use actual days in the month method for proration)?

A. $293.55 Debit Seller, $293.55 Credit Buyer
B. $1,006.45 Debit Seller, $1,006.45 Credit Buyer
C. $1,006.45 Debit Seller, $293.55 Credit Buyer
D. $1,006.45 Debit Seller, $293.55 Debit Buyer

14. A homeowner's property, in the city limits, has an assessed value of $244,000 and the county commissioners have just passed a horizontal adjustment of +12% for the upcoming tax year. If the county tax rate is .86 per 100 dollars of value and the city tax rate is .36 per $100 of value, what will be the total annual tax bill for the homeowner?

A. $2,098
B. $2,350
C. $2,997
D. $3,334

15. Using the Rectangular Survey System, how many acres would there be in the tract of land described as the NE 1/4 of the SW 1/4 of the SE 1/4 of Section 12 T4NR3W?

A. 10 acres
B. 40 acres
C. 64 acres
D. 640 acres

16. A tract of land that has a road frontage of 225 feet and a depth of 700 feet and is listed for $22,000 per acre. The land ultimately sold for $19,000 per acre. What was the sales price of the lot, rounded to the nearest hundred dollars?

A. $61,900
B. $68,700
C. $74,860
D. $86,700

17. An investor is trying to determine the value of an apartment complex and his research produces the following results: there are 40 units which rent for $900 per month. Vacancy in the local market averages 5% and expenses average $9,500 per month. The debt service on this property would be $17,000 per month. The investor's partners value properties using a 10% capitalization rate. What would be the value of this property using the income approach?

   A. $924,000
   B. $2,794,000
   C. $2,964,000
   D. $3,180,000

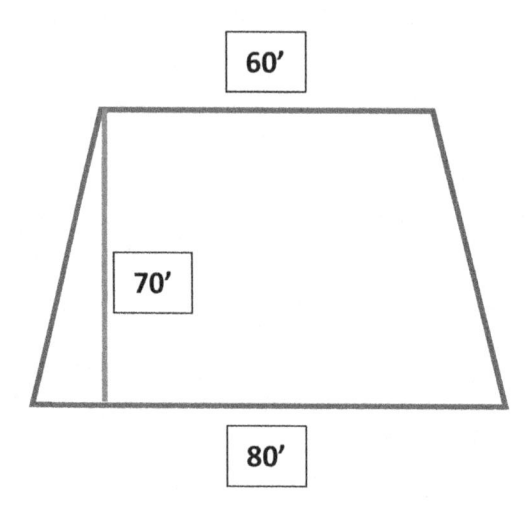

18. What is the square footage of the lot described above?

   A. 4,200
   B. 4,400
   C. 4,900
   D. 5,600

19. P owns a property that she is interested in selling. P contacts B to list the property and her partner J prepared a CMA. The subject property has 4BR, 3BA, a fireplace and a 1 car garage. J finds a comp that recently sold for $221,000 that sold 3 months ago, has 4BR, 2BA, no fireplace and a 2 car garage. A bathroom, is worth $7,500, fireplace $5,500, 1 car garage $4,500, 2 car garage $11,000 and appreciation of 5% for the year. What is the adjusted value of the property, rounded to the nearest hundred?

A. $217,300
B. $230,100
C. $230,300
D. $243,100

20. The 6% commission on a recent sale of $213,000 was divided equally between the buyer's agent and the seller's agent. The buyer's agent's firm has a policy of a 60% pay out to the agent after taking a 6% franchise fee. How much is the buyer's agent share of the compensation, rounded to the nearest dollar?

A. $2,428
B. $3,003
C. $3,604
D. $6,071

21. A particular property has 50 units which rent as follows: 36 units are 2 bedrooms and rent for $800 per month. The remaining units are 3 bedrooms and rent for $900 per month. All of the 2 bedrooms were occupied and 11 of the three bedrooms were occupied paying full price while one other unit was prorated for 13 days of rent for the month of June. The property manager charges a management fee of 8% of rent received. What would be the property manager's commission on this property for June, rounded to the nearest dollar?

A. $3,096
B. $3,127
C. $3,168
D. $3,312

22. A provisional broker is contacted to list a property where the seller desires to net $100,000 from the sale of the property. The current mortgage balance is $175,000, commission of 6%, deed preparation of $125 and other seller closing costs of $1,000. What must the property sell for in order for the seller to cover all expenses and net the desired amount?

A. $259,558
B. $260,495
C. $293,750
D. $295,558

23. Gena is purchasing a home for $145,000, obtaining a conventional mortgage with 95% loan to value. She is weighing two loan options, a 15-year loan at 4% interest with a factor of 7.40 or a 30-year loan at 4 ½% interest with a factor of 5.07. How much interest would Gena save by selecting the 15-year loan, rounded to the nearest hundred?

A. $67,900
B. $71,500
C. $124,000
D. $130,500

24. Otto is purchasing a home for $293,000 with an assessed value equal to 80% of the purchase price. The local municipality charges 14 Mills. The closing is scheduled for October 19th and the taxes are unpaid for the year. The attorney will charge both the buyer and seller their portion of the taxes and pay it at closing. How much will the buyer pay if they agree to pay for the day of closing?

A. $3,281.60
B. $2,625.28
C. $ 820.40
D. $ 656.32

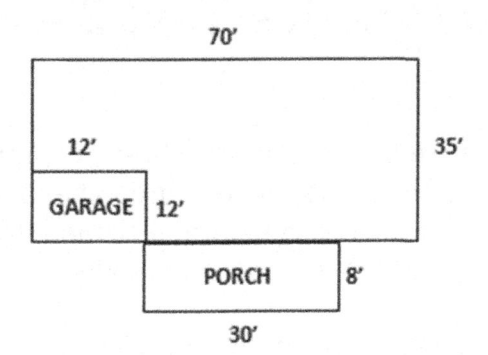

25. Based on the drawing above, what is the living area square footage of this single-story home?

A. 2,690
B. 2,546
C. 2,450
D. 2,306

Math Practice Test 2 – Solution

1. A - $2,420.   The first step is to determine the maximum amount of housing expenses and total expenses that the buyer can have and still qualify for the mortgage. Next you subtract the long-term recurring obligations from total debt. The maximum PITI payment will be the lower of the two.

   Monthly Income: ($50,000 + $60,000) ÷ 12 = $9,167
   Maximum housing: $9,167 X 28% = $2,567
   Maximum total debt: $9,167 X 36% = $3,300
   Maximum total debt less recurring expenses: $3,300 - $630 - $250 = $2,420

2. D - $4,875. The first step to determine the minimum income needed to qualify, is to break expenses into two categories – housing expenses and housing expenses plus recurring obligations. Divide housing expenses by 28%. Divide housing expenses and recurring obligations by 36%. The minimum income is the higher of the two numbers. Make sure to read the problem carefully as they may ask for monthly or yearly income.

   Housing obligations: $925 + $250 = $1,175
   Housing expenses and recurring obligations: $1,175 + $580 = $1,755
   Minimum income housing: $1,175 ÷ 28% = $4,196
   Minimum income total debt: $1,755 ÷ 36% = $4,875

3. B - $115,497. When calculating the total interest that has been paid over the life of the loan, take the monthly payment and multiplied by the number of payments that will be made, then subtract the original amount borrowed. When comparing two loans where the borrower's mortgage is for the same amount, there is no need to back out the original loan amount.

   Total principal and interest 30-year mortgage: $1,229.85 X 360 = $442,746
   Total principal and interest 15-year mortgage: $1,818.05 X 180 = $327,249
   Total interest saved: $442,746 – $327,249 = $115,497

4. C - $38,402.39. It is important to read the problem to determine whether your calculating how much the seller will net from the sale or how much the buyer will need to bring to closing. Recall that the seller typically pays CD&E - commission, deed prep and excise tax.

Sales Price	$185,000.00
- Loan	-148,000.00 ($185,000 X 80%)
+ Discount points	+1480.00
+ Origination fee	+585.00
+ Interim interest	+164.44 ($148,000 X 5% ÷ 360 X 8 days)
- Property tax	-322.05 ($1,026 ÷ 360 X 113 Days – DR S CR B)
+ Property insurance	+600.00
+ Attorney fee	+725.00
+ Title insurance	+370.00
- Due diligence fee	-200.00
- Earnest money deposit	-2,000.00
Net from Buyer	$38,402.39

5. C - $1,037,500. First calculate the cost of the building new. When calculating the value of a property using the cost approach make sure that you use the effective age to determine depreciation rather than actual age. Depreciation is calculated by taking the new value and dividing by the economic life, then multiplying by the effective age. Next add in the value of land and improvements.

    Building new: 3,500 X $300 = $1,050,000
    Depreciation: $1,050,000 ÷ 60 X 15 = $262,500
    Property value: $1,050,000 - $262,500 + $250,000 = $1,037,500

6. D - $242,000. The first step is adding up the known seller expenses, which is excludes commission. Commission is based on the sales price, see you cannot multiply by the lower figure by the commission rate to determine the sales price. In this example commission is 6%. The sales price is 100% - commission of 6% = 94%. Divide the known seller net and expenses by this percent to determine the sales price.

    Known net and expenses: $50,000 +$175,000 + $2,500 = $227,500
    Sales price needed: $227,500 ÷ 94% = $242,021.27, rounded $242,000

7. C - $203,175. Only adjust the comparable property, never the subject property. When a comparable property is inferior we increase. When a comparable property is superior we subtract. When calculating appreciation, it is often quoted for the year so make sure to divide by 12 and multiply by the number of months from when the comp sold.

Subject	Comparable -	$190,000
3 BR	3BR	-
2 Full BA	1 Full BA	+ 2,500
No .5 BA	1 .5 BA	-1,500
2,000 SQFT	2,050 SQFT	-1,250 (50 X $25)
1 Car Gar	1 Car Gar	-
FP	No FP	+ 1,000
No Patio	Patio	-4,000
$15K Upgrade	No Upgrade	+ 15,000
	Appreciation	+1,425 ($190,000 X 3% ÷ 12 X 3)
	ADJUSTED	$203,175

8. B - 28.6%. You must first calculate the amount of the gain by taking the sales price and subtracting the purchase price. Next divide that amount by the original purchase price.

   Gain: $225,000 - $175,000 = $50,000
   Percentage gain: $50,000 ÷ $175,000 = 28.6%

9. B - 120. The gross rent multiplier is calculated by taking the sales price and dividing by the monthly rent. The gross income multipliers calculate by taking the sales price and dividing by annual rent.

   GRM: $150,000 ÷ $1,250 = 120

10. A - $163.33. Mortgage payments are due on the first of the month and recall that interest is paid in arrears. When a buyer assumes a mortgage, they will be responsible for the payment on the first of the following month. In this example closing occurred on June 12, so the buyer would have to pay the mortgage on July 1. It is common practice for the seller to pay through the day of closing, and less a problem states otherwise.

    Accrued interest: $140,000 X 3.5% ÷ 360 X 12 Days = $163.33

11. D - $244,647. When amortizing a loan make sure that you are just using the principal and interest portion of the payment. The only way to determine the change in the borrower's loan balance is to determine the interest for the month and then calculate the principal portion of the payment.

PI payment: $1,470 - $300 = $1,170
Monthly interest: $245,000 X 4% ÷ 12 = $816.67
Principal payment: $1,170 - $816.67 = $353.33
New balance: $245,000 - $353.33 = $244,646.67. rounded $244,647

12. B – Max Housing $1,960. Sometimes these questions will require you to answer I Only, II Only, Both or Neither. The test has minimized the use of this style of question. The answer choices here can feel overwhelming. Take a deep breath and read each answer option before answering.

    We need to determine the maximum amount of housing expenses and maximum amount of housing expenses and other obligations the buyer can have and still qualify. First convert the income into a monthly amount. Multiply monthly income by 28% for housing and 36% for total debt - this is the maximum amount. Now calculate the amount of housing expenses and housing expenses plus long-term debt. Compare these numbers to the maximum amount; if it is at or lower than the maximum than the buyer qualifies.

    Monthly income: $84,000 ÷ 12 = $7,000
    Maximum housing expenses: $7,000 X 28% = $1,960
    Actual housing expenses: $1,800 QUALIFIES
    Maximum total debt: $7,000 X 36% = $2,520
    Actual total debt: $1,800 + $800 = $2,600 DOES NOT QUALIFY

13. A - $293.55 - debit seller, credit buyer. It is important to remember that a seller is paid through the day of closing unless the problem states otherwise. Also use caution as this problem states that it is based on the actual days in the month. The seller has been paid for the entire month. This is not fair to the buyer, so they must credit money back to the buyer for the number of days of the buyer will own the property during that month.

    Daily rent: $1,300 ÷ 31 days = $41.9354
    Days to buyer: 31 – 24 = 7 days
    Rent proration amount: $41.9354 X 7 = $293.55

14. D - $3,334. A horizontal adjustment is an across-the-board tax increase. Take the assessed value and multiply it by 100% plus a percentage increase. A property that is located in the city will pay both city and county taxes. A property that is located in the County will only pay county taxes.

New assessed value: $244,000 X 112% = $273,280
Tax for year: $273,280 ÷ 100 X $1.22 = $3,334

15. A – 10 acres. There are 640 acres and a section. While this problem does not contain another lot, other test questions may include another description or state and X acres - which would require you to add.

    Acres: 640 ÷ 4 ÷ 4 ÷ 4 = 10

16. B - $68,700. In order to calculate acreage it is important to remember that there are 43,560 ft.² in an acre. One way to remember this, is 4 blue haired ladies driving 35 in a 60.

    Acres: 225' X 700' ÷ 43,560 = 3.6157
    Sales price: 3.6157 acres X $19,000 = $68,698.34, rounded $68,700

17. C - $2,964,000. When calculating the value of a building using the income capitalization approach, recall that the formula is net operating income divided by the capitalization rate. Net operating income is a G.I.V.E.N. Gross income less vacancy and collection less operating expenses equals net operating income. You do not include depreciation, debt service or capital improvements.

Gross income	$432,000 (40 units X $900 X 12 months)
-Vacancy	-21,600 ($432,000 X 5%)
Effective Gross Income	$410,400
-Operating expenses	-114,000 ($9500 X 12 months)
Net Operating Income	$296,400

    Value: $296,400 ÷ 10% = $2,964,000

18. C – 4,900 square feet. To calculate the area of a trapezoid recall the formula:
    ½ (Base 1 + Base 2) X Height

    Square Footage: ½ (60 + 80) X 70 = 4,900

19. C - $230,300. Only adjust the comparable property, never the subject property. When a comparable property is inferior we increase. When a comparable property is superior we subtract. When calculating appreciation, it is often quoted for the year so make sure to divide by 12 and multiplied by the number of months from when the comp sold.

Subject	Comparable -	$221,000
4 BR	4BR	-
3 Full BA	2 Full BA	+ 7,500
FP	No FP	+ 5,500
1 Car Gar	No 1 Car Gar	+4,500
No 2 Car Gar	2 Car Gar	-11,000
	Appreciation	+2,763 ($221,000 X 5% ÷ 12 X 3)
	ADJUSTED	$230,263 , rounded $230,300

20. C - $3,604. The franchise fee is calculated prior to splitting the money between the brokerage and the agent. You can calculate the 6% and subtract it out or as a shortcut multiply 94%.

    Commission per brokerage: $213,000 X 6% ÷ 2 = $6,390
    Buyers agent share: $6,390 X 94% X 60% = $3,603.96, rounded $3,604

21. B - $3,127. Property management fees are typically charged on the rent received, as it is stated in the problem. Therefore, you must prorate rent for the one unit that is only rented for 13 days.

    Two-bedroom rent: 36 units X $800 = $28,800
    Three-bedroom rent: 11 units X $900 = $9,900
    Prorated rent: $900 ÷ 30 X 13 days = $390
    Total June rent collected: $28,800 + $9,900 + $390 = $39,090
    Management fee: $39,090 X 8% = $3,127.20, rounded $3,127

22. C - $293,750. The first step is adding up the known seller expenses, which excludes commission. Commission is based on the sales price, so you cannot multiply the lower figure by the commission rate to determine the sales price. In this example commission is 6%. The sales price is 100% - commission of 6% = 94%. Divide the known seller net and expenses by this percent to determine the sales price.

    Known net and expenses: $100,000 +$175,000 + $150 + $1,000 = $276,125
    Sales price needed: $276,125 ÷ 94% = $293,750

23. A - $67,900. In order to determine the amount of interest that will be saved when comparing one loan to the other, you must know the monthly principal and interest payment. You then multiply the monthly payment by the number of payments to determine the total principal and interest paid. Then you calculate the difference. The mortgage payment will be based on the loan amount not to purchase price.

    Loan amount: $145,000 X 95% = $137,750
    Payment 30 YR: $137,750 ÷ 1,000 X 5.07 = $698.39
    Total payments 30 YR: $698.39 X 360 = $251,421.30
    Payment 15 YR: $137,750 ÷ 1,000 X 7.40 = $1,019.35
    Total payments 15 YR: $1,019.35 X 180 = $183,483
    Interest Saved: $251,421.30 - $183,483 = $67,938.30, rounded $67,900

24. D - $656.32. When the buyer will pay the taxes for the day of closing, calculate the number days the month similar to interim interest by adding a day. Property taxes are based on the assessed value and not the sales price. Since were dealing with mills the assessed value should be divided by a thousand.

    Assessed value: $293,000 X 80% = $234,400
    Taxes for year: $234,400 ÷ 1,000 X 14 mils = $3,281.60
    Daily rate of tax: $3281.60 ÷ 360 = $9.1155
    Days: N (30-19+1) 12 + ND 60 = 72 Days Buyer
    Buyer charge: $9.1155 X 72 days = $656.32

25. D – 2,306 square feet. Living area must be heated, finished and directly accessible. A garage and porch are not considered living area.

    Large rectangle: 70' X 35' = 2,450
    Garage: 12' X 12' = 144
    Living area: 2,450 – 144 = 2,306

ACKNOWLEDGEMENTS

We would like to thank Chris Barnette for his contributions to this workbook. Chris is a real estate instructor in North Carolina, teaching prelicense, postlicense and continuing education courses.

ABOUT THE AUTHORS

Matt Davies is a North Carolina real estate instructor and began teaching in 2008. He is an active real estate broker and obtained his broker license in 2003. Matt teaches prelicense, postlicense and continuing education courses using multiple approaches to help students understand difficult topics. Matt has a Bachelor of Science in Business Administration with a concentration in Accounting from Bryant University. Prior to entering real estate, Matt worked for PricewaterhouseCoopers LLP.

Doug is a North Carolina real estate professional and licensed real estate instructor who brings a wealth of knowledge and experience to help navigate the real estate market. He has advanced degrees in Mathematics and Communications from Florida State University and Boston University, and an undergraduate degree in Landscape Architecture from the University of Massachusetts – Amherst. His background of over 25 years in marketing in high tech and management consulting enables him to convey difficult concepts to his students.

Tiffany R. Ross has been educating students of all ages for many years, and has recently become an instructor for real estate prelicensing, postlicensing and continuing education. Tiffany obtained a Bachelor of Science in Industrial Engineering from Florida State University, with a minor in Mathematics, and continued to get her Masters of Science in Industrial & Systems Engineering from Georgia Institute of Technology, before getting licensed in 2001. Tiffany is committed to improving students success and confidence by simplifying math concepts.

North Carolina
Comprehensive Review
2019 - 2020

Matt Davies
Tiffany Ross

First Edition

Coming Soon

www.3WiseTeachers.com

North Carolina Real Estate
State Only Exam Review
2019 - 2020

Matt Davies
Tiffany Ross

Third Edition

Coming Soon

www.3WiseTeachers.com

www.LearnTestPass.com

Join the course for FREE - to access 25-Question Exam

Additional Resources Available For Purchase.

Free 25 Question Math Exam—Just visit the site—set up an account and you have unlimited assess. (Shameless Promotion Alert): There are additional resources—National and NC State Exams available for purchase at reasonable prices. You get exam worthy questions with detailed explanations.

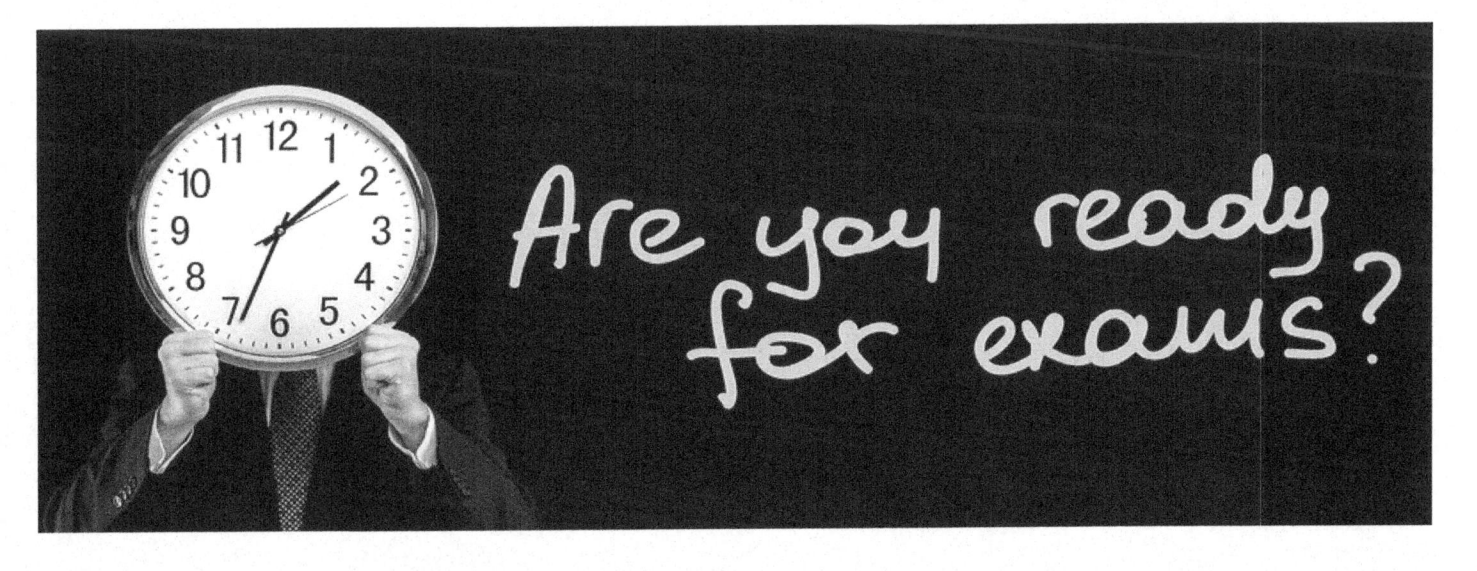

Are you ready for exams?

Made in the USA
Coppell, TX
30 January 2020